BRICK, CEMENT & DOTCOM

the unspoken dark realities of entrepreneurship

deep malhotra

Brick, Cement & Dotcom

The Unspoken Dark Realities Of Entrepreneurship

Deep Malhotra

Invincible Publishers

Published by
Invincible Publishers
201A, SAS Tower, Sector 38, Gurugram – 122003
Phone: +91-124-4034247, +91 9355675555
www.i-publish.in

This book is a work of fiction inspired by true events in the author's life. Names, characters, places and incidents are either withheld or the product of the author's imagination or are used fictitiously. Any resemblance to real persons, living or dead, or actual events or locations, is purely coincidental and the publisher does not hold responsibility for the same.

First Published in 2020

ISBN: 978-93-89600-90-2

Dedicated to my Dad & Mom, my sister Sonali & my wife Shikha, without whom this journey wouldn't have been possible & worthwhile.

PS: Thanks to my wife who challenged & then threatened me to use the lockdown to write the book I always wanted to; "If I didn't write it now, it meant I had never been serious about it." So, blame her if you don't like the book.

Contents

Introduction	8
Passion Is Overrated	12
Going Digital	18
Don't Sell, Be Sold	28
Journey: An Employee To An Entrepreneur	34
Are You Just Another Jack?	42
Be Lean	50
Lessons By Dad	58
Victims or Villains Of Real Estate	64
Dealing With The Different Worlds	70
Just A Brick In The Wall	78
A Thriller Called Startup	84
Play The Hand You Are Dealt	94
Approximation In Business Building	100
What They Never Told Us	106
WTF Forty	114
You Are As Good As Your Bad Habits	124
The Dark Side	130
No Entry - For The Unsuccessful !!!	138
End Of The World Or Just Another Day	144
'Living The Moment' Makes You What You Are!	152
Half Time To Goal Time	158
Epilogue	166

Introduction

"*If you want to make the money you think you deserve, then you should do this project on your own,*" advised the senior executive of one of the Mumbai's biggest real estate firms as I walked out of his cabin with my dad, all confused and dejected. Those 20 minutes in that cabin in the year 2009 changed many things for me in the next decade; it gave me a reality check that helped me a long way. I feel that in life, there are only a few moments like these that define you and make you what you are in the end.

When I look back on my career, from being a teenage part-time graphic designer in the late 1990s to having been an amateur entrepreneur who failed amid the dot - com bubble burst and later being associated with big tech companies, I realize I was ultimately destined to get into real estate development and consciously diversify further into co-working spaces and funding technology startups in 2020. It has truly been a rollercoaster ride with twists and turns on the path ahead. How I had dealt with certain moments in my life with hindsight has taken me where I am today.

In this book, I would like to talk about the moments which changed things for me and the learning and experiences gained in the ride of turning from an employee into an entrepreneur. There are many dark realities that most don't like to talk about when setting up a business, with the much drama and myths around running your own company. The journey of working in multiple and strikingly different industries of technology, media, and real estate has given me invaluable insights into human behavior and how to deal with situations in building your business as an entrepreneur.

My experience has taught me that there is a difference in being an Entrepreneur and being Entrepreneurial. On the surface, they may sound the same things, but they aren't always the same. Being an entrepreneur is something that is in vogue nowadays. It definitely gives you a high to see the word of the CEO affixed with your name on the visiting card and there are indeed some upbeat things that go with the tag of an entrepreneur. Also, everyone likes to hear a good story, especially with a happy ending. But behind the story, the episodes of being entrepreneurial are not always spoken about. It doesn't always involve gleeful things, and there is this consistent hustling, the sleepless nights, and the list goes on. These tough tales actually make us real entrepreneurs. And this is the real face of entrepreneurship, because acting as an entrepreneur may look glamorous and exciting from outside, but being entrepreneurial every day isn't rose-colored and is sometimes very dark too.

We, the entrepreneurs have many such dark days and darker nights when we are alone fighting the inky realities of being entrepreneurial. I hope you enjoy reading the ups and downs in my journey of entrepreneurship that I am going to uncover through this book.

PostScript: Don't miss the Post Scripts at the end of each chapter!

CHAPTER 1

Passion Is Overrated

I am sure many of you won't agree with me on the title of this chapter. I have seen a lot of talks, presentations, and discussions around how Passion is the fuel for a successful startup. But I disagree. Passion is certainly a key ingredient, but it is not the only one that is important.

It is said - When you do something you love, you do not have to work anymore. Reality is - When you make a business out of something you love, you have to do certain other things in addition that you may not love so much (or at all, at times). Now, this is totally different when you are not doing it for business - Who would care if you are making money out of it or not? Because, ultimately, you are having fun doing what you love.

My point is - Passion wears off in a few months after you start your venture which was based on your passion; because you are no longer doing it for fun, but to build something which is profitable for you and others associated with it. Pressure builds up and sooner or later, you question yourself if this was what you really loved and if you did, then why did you make it into a business?

Passion alone wasn't enough to survive in my first venture: It was the year 1998, the time when I, an 18 - year - old, was slowly trying to understand the power of digital media through the then newly introduced world wide web in India. Already equipped with a few design courses in the previous couple of years, I was sure my career would be all about graphic and web design in the future. I started my digital design career when I was in junior college, as a part-time designer for a few popular magazines. Soon I had a hunch that I have to start something of my own; something in the growing new media space. In 2000, just a year before the dot - com bubble burst impact in India, I launched my first venture called Onmag.com - an online creativity magazine allowing creative people to display their talent on the platform. The business was built as an online fortnightly magazine publishing content from amateur writers, photographers, and designers. The magazine was made to showcase the talent and in turn, provide talent to various media houses. Other than this, there were advertising opportunities for brands on the web which targeted the youth. Driven with passion, I ran its operations for 24 months, till the venture met its end due to lack of external funding, similar to the most dotcom businesses bursting at that time.

But, what I had learned in running this eventually unsuccessful business was that you are responsible for a lot more things than just the core business, especially when you're the one running the show. A business requires you to take care of a lot of things like investment, the attrition rate of your employees, payment collections, monthly bills, monthly salaries, etc. And, maybe these are not the things you are passionate about. The actual passion and the core of it slowly take the backseat.

This brings us to one of the most underrated terms that we seldom hear from the experts, forums, and conferences related to startups - I believe that term is Persistence. Because just loving what you do is not enough to make it into a successful business. You need the Persistence to make it big! 'Why?' 'Well, because it isn't easy to build a business - a lot of crazy things happen out there during the process. And to sustain it, it takes a lot out of you.' You might be surprised that the thing you loved doing just for fun isn't fun anymore because the business and the humdrum around it took the fun out of it; except when you really love running a business, since in that case you actually love the challenges thrown at you. Then, it doesn't matter what kind of business you are in until it is growing and making money.

So, Passion is actually overrated and Persistence is a bigger requirement than Passion in building a successful startup. Just because passion sounds sexier and pumps out more adrenaline rush than persistence, we give it more importance. But any entrepreneur who has been at least six months into his/her business would tell you passion isn't the only fuel that is helping drive the business, especially when he/she is not making the revenue expected.

In the end, Passion can definitely help you kickstart your startup but Persistence is needed to run it. Hence, do remember this as a fact that Persistence is equally or more important than your Passion in building your business, and keeping it alive!

❖❖❖

PostScript 1: I started my career as a part-time graphic designer with CHIP Magazine in the late 1990s. Along with that, I used to take up a lot of graphic and web design freelance work on the side. Many times I was short paid for my freelance work, not because the client didn't like the design but because he thought the work was done too quickly. This drilled in my head that people don't value the work if it is done, even efficiently, before time. Also, if you turn around things at the last moment, you are considered a savior. Building on this made me work more effectively in the last moment of chaos. Maybe, it isn't the right thing to follow but it has worked for me many times.

CHAPTER 2

Going Digital

In the year 2005 at an industry conclave, where we were discussing how traditional media agencies don't get the power of going digital, acting as gatekeepers to let big clients use it effectively. I was told by an industry veteran that in 18 months from then, all that would change as we were approaching the tipping point of digital media. The tide was to turn in our favor. It made me excited and equally proud of choosing my career in digital advertising back then.

Pumped up with that confidence, the next day, in a meeting with the marketing head and his team of one of the top global FMCG clients, I walked into the conference room as if I owned the place. The only reason I could get in a meeting with this top-notch company was that the company I represented was an enigma back then called Google and I was amongst the rare couple of people in India who were responsible for setting up the company's direct sales operation in the country back then. So, being in the founding team for Google India carried quite a weighty responsibility on me and it also opened many tough, opportunistic doors for me too.

The people in the room were bombarded with a colorful presentation of the digital ad formats, internet statistics, and the reasons why digital advertising is way much cooler than any other form of advertising. The marketers in the room tried to digest the new information presented to them, including confusing acronyms like CTR (Click Through Rate), CPC (Cost Per Click) and CPL (Cost

Per Lead). I wasn't sure if many understood what was presented, but they were possibly too embarrassed to ask numerous questions. I guess at that time digital spending was a very small percentage of the overall advertising spending for a brand, so the interest level to know about digital advertising by the marketing team was directly proportional to the spending they did.

Nevertheless, the marketing head was nodding throughout the presentation, and after a yawn or two in the middle, he disclosed that his total budget for a digital marketing campaign was Rs. 10 lakh, which was a big budget for a single brand to spend at that time. He agreed to part with half of it on a CPC (cost per click) model that was proposed by me. But he wanted at least Rs. 5 per response as the metric for the campaign. I shook hands with him on the sealed deal, shut my laptop, and walked out the cabin with a fulfilling feeling of achievement.

Both sides were content. I was closer to my quarterly target; the marketing head was elated because he could count 100,000 hits on his soon - to - be - launched brand microsite. The question is: If both sides were happy, why is there a problem in how digital advertising was sold?

To understand this better, let's look back to what led the marketing head to call me to his office back then. He was under pressure from their international headquarters to allocate a certain portion of their budget to the digital activities because apparently, their competition had just disclosed how well the internet has worked for them for their new product launch. And then, of course, none of the brands wanted to be outdated by not adopting digital advertising. So, the marketing head planned to have the mandate to allocate some percentage of his marketing spends on digital advertising. And that's when the call was taken to add 'digital' in the marketing budget. After spending some years in the business, I later realized the mistakes we made in selling this medium to our advertisers:

Digital advertising was always an afterthought in the media plan: Usually, the digital portion was expected to be within the limits of the residual marketing budget, after allocation of the spending in television, print, radio, and even outdoor advertising. Usually, the digital spend was a small percentage of the overall marketing budget, hence advertisers didn't bother with its execution until the very end. One reason for this could also be that the digital has always been sold as an 'easy to go and live with' medium. As opposed to this, the thought is: Why bother about the execution till the very end? Digital was almost never a part of the overall brand strategy and was treated more like one among the last - moment frills.

We try to over complicate the medium with complex metrics: Ask a hundred digital sales executives, 'What is one of the biggest strengths of digital advertising?' I bet the maximum answers would be, 'It helps you track your ROI till the very last penny spent with metrics like CPC, CPL, CPA (Cost Per Action).' I feel that due to this perception, it has become one of the biggest weaknesses for the medium because marketers only look for ROI through clicks received or leads generated and leave other important things like brand building catered to a glamorous medium like television or print. This is because marketers and digital sales executives do not usually speak the same language.

We try to de - sell other mediums to upsell ourselves making us fall flat on our face: *"Half the money I spend on advertising is wasted; the trouble is I don't know which half,"* even holds true today as said by John Wanamaker (1838 - 1920), a very successful United States merchant and a political figure, considered by some to be a pioneer in marketing. Now if digital executives think the biggest strength of digital advertising is tracking spends, then their easiest pitch would be to de - sell any medium that cannot do this efficiently. But this has been tried and tested, with limited success. Advertising isn't only about tracking spends, but about building brands. This is not known to many and maybe that's why there are not many examples of brands built solely through digital advertising till very recently.

We do not look beyond our circle: There are two kinds of marketers for us - those who have a digital background and understand the medium; the rest don't. The problem is that usually, those who do not have the digital background are the ones sitting with a bigger chunk of money for the brand building, who generously spend on so-called traditional media. Unfortunately, for us, these two kinds of marketers have taken time to come together, and hence now is when we see digital advertising spends are starting to reach its 'tipping point'. We need more such marketers soon to ride on the next wave of digital advertising.

The industry structure is too complex: We have digital design agencies, search marketing folks, social media experts, numerous ad networks, etc. and others; the structure is very complex, seldom connected, and that puts advertisers off. Usually, the brand appoints its lead agency to hire these smaller agencies, on the basis of who bids the lowest for the clicks or likes or leads, which are traded as commodities. All this is done for the sake of extending a client's offline campaign online, which is commonly considered as 'integration of media'.

These are some of the missteps made in the process of selling the digital in India. The matter can be solved but the first step towards doing that is to agree that there is indeed a problem. I am not sure how many people will agree that we have a problem with the way we look at the digital platform and its impending capacity. It is easier to blame the marketing heads, brand managers, or traditional agencies who do not allow digital advertising spends to increase as the gatekeepers.

Few factors that make digital advertising indispensable:

Right Creative Approach: A digital campaign is often a mere replication of the offline campaign of the brand. Developing or enabling creative talent that understands the technology and its high engagement proficiently may be one of the answers to get things right in the first place.

Integration: Digital strategies are usually thought of as separate from the overall marketing strategy, making it apart from the media mix. Many brands have successfully integrated digital strategies into the overall strategy, also on the international platform. When 'Digital' is the center point of your marketing strategy, you can't really run away from spending on it.

In 2009, the digital platform wasn't a blue-eyed medium to put your money with and after leaving Google and joining MySpace, I knew it isn't going to be easy to sell ads on MySpace, as Google had a robust product, AdWords which was focused on high return on investment, thus making it very performance-centric. Hence, selling on social media back then was the challenge to give the same advertisers their money's worth. To break this, we built 360 degree integrated plans for the advertisers, which included rock shows, movie premieres, and entertainment shows for the users going online, so as to let them interact with the brand; as well as giving the brands a taste of events, televised shows, and new media packed into one. This was in a true sense, integration of media for brands back then. But we couldn't experiment much with it as Facebook killed the MySpace party worldwide with a better engaging product for the long run.

The Collective Approach: The Digital is a complex medium, and it cannot be handled like any other medium. It requires time. It is ever-evolving and the parameters of a successful campaign keep changing. It is easy to blame the agency or the platform used for not getting the expected success in a short period. So, it is really important to work together to dissect this complex medium to get the maximum return on investment from it. Just by adding digital as a last-minute frill won't help, as then, we would not unleash the true potential of the medium.

These are just a few factors that, I feel, have set the ball rolling faster and brought us to the start of the journey towards the tipping point in digital media today.

❖❖❖

PostScript 2: Though the things may be different now in the digital media industry and many won't agree with me but the path we have taken to reach there wasn't the precise one as the whole running behind the 'Cost Per Click' and 'You Pay Only If It Works' model didn't actually leave ample opportunity space for the digital platform to be taken seriously for brand building. Things could've moved at a faster pace and digital could've been more of a brand-building medium, other than just a click & lead-based one it had been earlier. I have always been passionate about digital advertising that explains my choice of going for the lower salary package from Rediff.com on the campus vs the more lucrative one in a consumer-facing company after completing my Masters In Advertising & Communication from Symbiosis Institute of Business Management, Pune. I remember my debate in the late - 2005, with a marketing head of a top car brand, who was adamant that digital will never replace the television in brand building, wherein my over-enthusiasm and self - appointed advocacy for digital, I re-quoted that within 18 months things will be different. After 20 months or so, he was still allocating only 10% of his total new brand launch budget on digital and wanted just clicks and leads from it rather than brand building. The truth is that for some categories of products and services, things didn't move that quickly to digital advertising.

CHAPTER 3

Don’t Sell, Be Sold

It was *7:45 pm* on the clock, a quiet conference room buzzed with notepads on the table in front of all. It had been over 10 minutes since anyone spoke in the room before the most important person in the room said it in a loud authoritative voice, "Eighty - Five"... the other side of the table asserts, "Ninety - Five"... And in response, a big shot agency executive weighs in again, "Ninety"... after which I uttered the three most beautiful words on this planet for the sales people, "Okay, let's close!" All get up for the final customary handshakes and pleasantries, having closed the deal for 90 Lacs which was almost 80% of the total digital spends planned by the brand for the campaign. Of Course, for me, it solely meant completing the last quarter sales target of the year smoothly yet again, for the third consecutive year now. However, a week back, the situation wasn't that bright as the same agency executive was allowing only a small percentage of the ad budgets for the campaign. But, when I opted to go and meet the client directly, the numbers tilted in our favor.

I guess that assertiveness has helped me build the business for the companies I have worked with, though it was the time when digital marketing was on the upswing and great sellable products were emerging which helped track responses effectively and made things easy too. But coming from a business family, I always believed in doing my job with an entrepreneurial fervor and that has made a difference. I have always believed in a simple principle of sales that if you know how to sell, you will never starve and would live happily. This made me understand the important ingredients for the whole selling process, which are usually less focused on:

Pre-empting: A good salesman always knows what is needed before he or she even knocks on a door to sell. Most people undervalue the power of pre-empting the situation in a sales pitch. Stimulating multiple scenarios in your head beforehand helps since ultimately, we all know, it takes more of the mind over matter to close a deal. Selling is like a game of chess; to win you need to think at least one step ahead of the person across the table.

Relationships: Even if you are making lower margins, make sure you build strong relationships that average out your loss (es) in the long term. A good salesman achieves numbers while a good dealmaker wins favors; it's always a choice between short term goals and that of the long term. I prefer people owing me favors than money because money is cheap while favors are priceless. Always invest in relationships, it would ensure you'll get better returns.

Integrity: Let's get this right - Selling ice to an Eskimo isn't great selling, it is actually fleecing. It is important that you sell 'a solution' to 'the problem' before you add the other stuff. If you know your product or service won't be useful to the client, don't sell it. Because, if it is a one-sided sale, it might happen only one time. A successful deal is when both sides win, creating more potential opportunities.

Impact: The first impression lasts till the end. Usually, when the other side gets back first after a sales pitch, your chances of winning the deal gets high. Follow-ups are overrated, so avoid it till it is really required. If you have pitched it right the first time, you only need ten percent of the persuasion afterward. Success in sales isn't just about creating money; it is more about creating an impact. Usually, my most successful sales pitches were the shortest. I remember pitching Google Adwords to the CMO of a new airline; the pitch lasted for about 15 minutes and ended with him allocating the majority of their advertising budget to us.

YES: Every crisis is an opportunity waiting to be changed. Similarly, the way I see it, every 'NO' you get from the other side is an opportunity in disguise for you to make the other side say 'YES' on something else. The key is to let the other side come on to finally saying what you want them to, and at times, de - selling your points work. In the end, a successful deal is all about getting the other side to agree with your perspective.

Poker Face: Sometimes it gets rough, but remember that just because you are loud while negotiating doesn't mean you are a good negotiator. The art is to put across your idea with a smile. In a negotiation, every action has an opposite reaction. Don't react to the reaction as it could take you in the opposite direction, towards a downfall; instead, keep moving ahead on your own path. When you are in a difficult situation, it's best to put up a poker face to beat the odds. The tactic to call out the other side's bluff is one of the best ones to make use of in a negotiation.

I have realized after my few years of stint in sales that a short experience on the negotiation table is far more powerful than the years of learning theory on the subject. Selling is a never - stopping cycle; you need to keep pedaling it from target to target. Eventually, how good was your ride depends on how many deals you could close by the time it ends. You can take a man out of sales, but you cannot take a salesman out of that man. So, keep selling and keep growing happily ever after.

Dedicated to all the sales folks out there, because everyone lives by selling something.

PostScript 3: Back in 2006, a small-time agency founder didn't have enough funds to activate a big ad campaign because their credit limit was low and a big advance amount was required to start it. Though he could arrange the amount in a week, he needed the campaign to start the next day, or else he would have lost the business. I took a cheque from him which I needed to send to my accounts department which, in turn, was in a different city. I delayed sending the cheque for 6 days and let the campaign sail through so that he could get expected funds into his bank account. In hindsight, it was a risk I took to get him the required business. Eventually, that small-time agency got sold to a big media agency. The company isn't that small-time anymore and in return, owes me a favor someday. Investing in relationships gets you better returns in the long run.

CHAPTER 4

Journey: An Employee To An Entrepreneur

I always went about doing my job like running my own venture. I was fearless in my approach. In 2009, my father had a stroke, though his recovery didn't take long, the aftermath gave me a reality check of sorts. I consciously started giving some time to his business in my free time after work to help my dad. We had a couple of building projects stuck in the middle due to pending approvals because of which cash flow in the business was trapped. The best way to get through this was by selling off a few units in the project to interested investors. With my selling experience coming in handy, we were fortunate to get some good deals, and in the next few months, funds were no longer a problem. The execution of the projects and sticking to the deadlines committed to the investor became the number one priority for us. Next year, I made a decision to take a sabbatical for 6 - 12 months and join my family business of real estate development. Little did I know that the decision taken at that time would change my life.

After being part of the digital world for a decade then, I knew that doing something completely different won't be easy. But, I was very wrong, it wasn't just tough but the most cutthroat and crazy industry I had gotten into - the Real Estate Industry. The thing is when you have been part of some of the biggest companies which run a multi-million dollar business, you think that you are actually the guy who is running the show and getting the revenues and that if you put yourself in any other situation or company, you will continue making these millions. This is untrue, especially in the case when it is something as hardcore as real estate. The idea behind joining my father's business was to get it on track in six to twelve months and then join back my cushy lifestyle of the senior management role in a well - known new media company. But I am now, more than 10 years into the business and still very much engaged in the business, having a time of my life and learning new things every day.

What actually happened? In the first 6 months of joining the business, I thought it was the worst thing that could have happened to me. More so, because I think the real estate business is one of the most unorganized and unprofessionally - run businesses that one can come across. Our company had four projects which were stalled for some reason or the other; one of which was a slum rehabilitation project with over 220 slum structures for over 1200 people to be rehabilitated. It was indeed a huge responsibility! This took me from having meetings and conferences in five - star hotels, where the media executives are usually found having meetings to the places where there is no proper ventilation or light and which have almost always more than 200 people gathered at a time, screaming at top of their lungs either at you or with you or for you. From meeting marketing heads, CEOs, and industry stalwarts to dealing with police, government officials, politicians, local goons and so-called social workers on a daily basis, it was similar to reality hitting you with a 100 kg hammer on your head.

This experience has helped me handle the

pressure of running an unorganized business in an unprofessional industry, raise capital in a cash crunch economy and also handle complex people who are cutthroat and unrelenting in their approach to get you out of business every single day. I realized that when people casually say that 'I want to do something of my own', most of the time they have no clue of what they are getting into. Being an entrepreneur may be a fad, but what goes into making one is not a joke. It's a glamorous thing to say that you got investor money and you are building this cool new business, which may not be necessarily making any money. The tough part is to make the business run on its own money.

My thoughts changed from that of being an employee to a business owner in the last decade; it made me realize your product, marketing plans, and revenue strategy can be thrown out of the window if your business is not making any money. When we look around ourselves, we don't see many successful startups because, I feel, the reason behind this is the business owners want to fly before they can walk. I have seen business plans with a projection of millions of customers before the business can even get ten customers. Forecasting and planning on magical tools like Microsoft Excel have no limits, you can project your company beating your competitor or being the number one company with a click of a button. But, realities are altogether different.

During this transition period from being an employee to a business owner, I have learned a few valuable lessons that helped me pave my journey:

It is easier to work for others than to be your own boss: Think about this, when you are an employee you don't have to bother about paying salaries or paying rent of the office or paying the vendors; life is smooth. What you care about is how & when you would complete your targets and how well you are getting paid in incentives. If you cannot handle the pressure of managing chaos, entrepreneurship just isn't for you.

Smaller things matter: The transition of the journey from an Employee to an Entrepreneur wasn't an easy one. For example: When you are working in an office as an employee your time flies by in a lot of unproductive activities like team lunches, the welcomes, farewells, even traveling from home to office, etc. So, even if you are in the office cutting a cake for a colleague, it is considered to be work. While when you are working on your own and especially when you are with a small team, you need to self - motivate yourself a lot as there isn't much that is going on till you make it happen. Both environs are different; each has its pros and cons. Being an entrepreneur, you need to make sure you are disciplined enough to follow the routine since if you'll take it easy, there is no one to pull you up to get you back on track.

Getting money from investors may sound glamorous, but the truth is way far from that: You might have heard this fairytale story, your friend's friend got this awesome idea for which he went to an investor who gave a million-dollar cheque for it and then, you anticipate that all of them lived happily ever after. But this friend from whom you had heard the story probably missed out the details on how & what his friend went through to get the cheque. So don't believe in such 'Once upon a time' fairytale stories. Get into details and make sure you are ready for the rigorous process of raising funds.

Combining your skill sets helps: In July 2011, my company launched our first In - house product Gemideals.com - a platform for real estate deals. What we wanted to do was to make real estate a more transparent & professional place. It made sense to combine my experience of working in technology companies with real estate and turn it into a fruitful business. Launching this product helped me understand the real estate market better as I could now get all disorganized and small brokers under one platform and they could use the platform as a professional and unified base. This also helped me in overcoming my shortcomings of joining the real estate business late as it gave us quick - time access to the real estate brokers in the market and helped in boosting sales phenomenally.

'People' are most important in business: When I was part of the Google India founding team, my profile extended to building and recruiting for the sales team, working with the HR team. One key thing that I have learned with my stint at Google, it is always important to hire people who are smarter than you, because they will always challenge you to do your best. It's critical to have a good founding team so that when you are expanding your team, you have better people building it. Good talent attracts only better talent. And you would never have to micromanage the people when you have the right talent which is empowered to excel.

PostScript 4: Toughest time for me in my transition period was the post lunchtime as when I was working as an employee, there were a lot of fun activities in office to do that one was not guilty of wasting time on. But, when you are in your own small office you are even guilty of being sleepy post-lunch. The toughest task for me in the transition period was to fight my sleep post-lunch; it may sound trivial but smaller things are usually the ones that are basal in your growth.

CHAPTER 5

Are You Just Another Jack?

The startup scene was buzzing in the year 2012. An industry visionary had said "It is not the experienced but a 21-22-year-old techie who will change the Indian startup ecosystem, as it needs new blood to bring the required change," and this stuck with me & my wife as neither of us was a techie or of that age anymore. So, I guess we didn't fit the criteria. Nevertheless, we wanted to make a difference. That made us start Gemini New Media Ventures - GNMV Spaces (www.imgemini.com) as a new media startup consultancy, co-working, and incubation firm.

I named the company with Gemini in it because my dad had started his brokerage firm before his marriage in the 1970s as 'Gemini Estate Agents', simply because Gemini was his sun sign. The interesting part was that he married my mom a few years after that who coincidently was also of same sun sign as his, i.e. Gemini, so he continued with naming the real development firm as Gemini Developers. Well, this doesn't stop here. I happened to be a Gemini as well and coincidentally, I married a Gemini too! So, I thought this name was perfect to carry on the legacy.

The idea behind starting Gemini New Media Ventures was to work with select young tech startup founders who were just out of college, to help them build their products and businesses around it. We had done tie-ups with many top technology institutes in the country to get access to such talents. This venture of mine made me come across many enthusiastic founders or I must say *Jacks,* who aspired to build their next 'Facebook' in no time and get to their billion-dollar valuation as if the investors were just waiting to hand out these valuations to their startups. There was a sense of entitlement in them which they thought the world needed to fulfill. It reminded me of the early days of the 2000 dot - com bubble burst.

The story of Jack: One day, out of the blue, Jack jumps out from his box and shouts out loud 'I don't want to live here anymore, I want to build my own Big Box'. Jack thought he didn't want to be just another Jack who lived in someone else's box - he wanted to be different. He had the passion and he thought in his mind, "What more does one need to build his own big box, besides the passion to build one?" So, when he jumped out of the old box he felt free, he felt excited, he knew he could now build a box of any size he wanted. And to no one's surprise, he chose big and set out to make the biggest box that anyone could think about. But there was one problem, Jack had never built a box before - he had only lived in it!

We see many startups making the same mistake as Jack who starts making the biggest box even before understanding how to make a box. There are certain key things that entrepreneurs miss out in the excitement of embarking on their journeys. I have come across such typical problems after interacting with many startups and going through their business plans while running my consultancy and co-working firm.

It's not always important to build the biggest box immediately: I have come across many business plans that aim at making the next big thing that could capture the entire market within 6 months.

I think it is important to prove your concept on a small level before you grow. It is prudent to test it out by getting a few users from your network before you even think about expanding it on the city scale. BIG isn't always powerful and small is sometimes more sensible, since the foundation needs consistent and small efforts, as well as a fairground for hit and trials before making it big. Hence, it is not always important to build the biggest box straight up, but something that grows and becomes a big business organically.

Is there a need for this box in the first place: Many entrepreneurs usually miss out on this key question: What is the need gap the product or service is trying to solve? This, I feel, is the single most important question that any business plan needs to answer. Most business plans I come across miss this big question or make the solution much more complex than it already might be.

Marketing can make your box look big, but it still might be empty: Most startups give more importance to marketing their product than making their product more robust and adept to solve the problem. Maybe that's why we see marketing spends on user acquisition by start-ups overpowering that of user acquisition through product excellence. Advertising spends on platforms such as Google & Facebook can be a bottomless pit and be addictive too in that case. But, 'Is it really building your brand?' is the big question, because when you stop the spending, your traffic on the website or app may drop drastically if the product isn't that sought - after.

Initially bootstrapping your box might make sense: If you are at a stage where you just have a prototype ready or in the making, then getting investor money for building your box may not always be the right thing to do. Investors aren't doing charity while investing in your dream - they need an exit and a profitable result. It is important to answer: What is the return on investment the investor can make after the business has achieved all that it has set out to do?

Living in a box may be tough but building your own box is tougher: Many entrepreneurs realize this sooner than later in their journey that maybe, working in a job is better than doing your own thing. Because building your own business takes a lot out of you. And that's usually when burnout happens and founders sway away from their focus.

Cheaper price for your box is not an innovation: Your product and service's cheaper price does not count in innovation. Because a cheaper option than yours will always throw you out of the market. In fact, it is always better to be in the premium space rather than have a cheaper differentiator model. Innovation is when you fracture the market place with your offering, where there is a clear benefit to the customer with your product or service and there is a big wedge between your product and what is already there in the market as an option.

We see many Jacks every day jumping out of

their old box, some make their own box while some are still trying. But there is one thing in common between all these Jacks that they are all driven to make their dream into a reality. With the current market scenario getting more challenging every day for every new box on the block, I hope the above few thoughts will help all the budding entrepreneurs in moving towards their dreams in a more realistic way. Because nothing is more beautiful & successful than having something you have built on your own which is long-lasting and creates a difference.

Dedicated to all the 'Jacks' who dream to create their own box.

❖❖❖

PostScript 5: You must have heard the story of a boy who claimed to know how to make the glug - glug machine, though he never could get even passing grades in his school time. But the school authorities always passed him to the next standard as he seemed smart and knew how to make a machine at a young age - only to know later that this machine did nothing but made the sounds of glug - glug when water was put in it. We have come across many such glug - glug machine inventors, few of which also got passing marks from investors to get to the next level, but then there was the realization that the machines didn't work and only made noise, till the plug was pulled out.

CHAPTER 6

Be Lean

Funding, funding everywhere but not a penny to invest in your startup! Well, that's what you feel when you are running a startup and usually run out of cash quickly. Several startups face this problem - they start out with enthusiasm and some funding from self, family, friends, or an angel to build out a perfect business, but end up spending too much, too soon.

Funds are important for your business to grow, but when you seek out an investor it is important to know that it isn't just about the money but it is also about getting a partner on board. It is important that there is a match of thoughts between the founders and the investors. It isn't necessary to agree on all things for both the parties but the basic fundamentals need to be in sync.

Usually, the investors bet on the basis of the people and if they find there is chemistry between their goals and yours, they would back you. Most businesses do not act as per the business plans they set out to go after, things change and you need to improvise as per the situation. That's when you realize the need of the right investor partner, the one who can bring common sense to the table of discussion.

For an investor, writing a cheque is an easy part but making sure things are on track is a tough one. The investor should be your sounding board in tough times. Weak people do not invest in tough times; therefore this is the pilot checkpoint for the winning conditions to be created. All thanks to risk capital or the venture capitals that we have expedited the progress in technology which has now helped us upgrade our standard of living. If we didn't have venture capitalists backing risky ideas we wouldn't have the semiconductor industry progressing into Silicon Valley as we know it today and breakthrough companies like Apple, Cisco, Intel to name a few. There is always a debate of what made them great, the companies, or the funds behind those great companies. But there is no use of having venture capital if there are no entrepreneurs with breakthrough ideas and ambitions, also with a fair amount of luck involved.

After 2 years of running Gemini New Media Ventures as the incubation for startups, helping the few startups to develop their business plans and figure their business models through our incubation program, we realized that the incubation model had a flaw since what we were trying to do was trying to standardize the process of building a business. We were quick to understand that we cannot use the learnings gained from running an education startup in scaling a health startup. It isn't a food dish that we prepare and so, there isn't a particular cookbook to build a startup; achieving it in batches of 6 - 8 weeks isn't the way to build it. Maybe the best way to build a business is to get your hands dirty on your own.

Understanding this, we moved from the incubation model to a co-working model for startups with benefits of consulting and support for growth under one roof, and that has worked well for us at

GNMV Spaces, which has made it grow from just 10 seat operations to 300+ seats in just a couple of years and now adding another 400 seats in a new setup to be completed in next 12 months.

Having worked with many startups, I realized that the funny thing about building a business is that the money, many assume, will suffice till the time they get the next batch of funding for their startup. Well, more often than not, founders need to take some harsh decisions to prematurely kill the startup due to lack of funds or they realize that pivoting the startup can be the way you can save it. But pivoting isn't easy if you have already burnt a lot of cash since every new strategy needs some money to back it up. Many founders tend to stick around with a broken model even when they know it isn't going anywhere because they have invested the investor's money and are too scared to take a chance and say that this isn't working.

In the enthusiastic race to make the game-changing product/business, startups tend to splurge the investor's money and this enthusiasm is reciprocated by the investor's inclination to build the next billion-dollar valuation. Ultimately, too much money is burnt too fast and before one realizes what is broken and how it can be fixed - the business is stuck between difficult choices of letting it go or changing the path.

Right now, the Indian startup ecosystem is gearing up for its next level. From being a small kid on the block we are getting onto a new phase. This phase does bring a lot of excitement and enthusiasm along with its share of problems. There are certain levels of caution that can help this ecosystem to thrive and make it strong to breed stronger startups which will stay for long. There are few areas where startups can keep a check on for a healthy future: -

Be microscopic in approach: Start small as big needs money. Prove your concept on a microscopic level before you grow. Test it out on 10 customers from your area before you even think about expanding it on the city scale. When the business is small, tweaks are easily possible and you can pivot it into an efficient business model if the one you started out with wasn't working. Try to prove your business model first.

Make money: You know what is cooler than 10,000 free users? 100 paying customers! There is nothing sweeter than making money before you expand. Many times, you see startups wanting to get insane valuation when they haven't even clocked in their first penny from their businesses.

Be frugal: This stands true even when you make it big with your venture. Getting funding isn't equal to winning a lottery ticket. The more frugal you are with your investor's money, the more confidence you will gain from the community.

Be understaffed: The best part of working in a startup is you get to do more than what is defined in your profile - hire people who agree to this statement and are ready to work in a similar fashion. Multi-tasking by your team members is an important ingredient for success. The smaller your team, the easier it is handled and pivoted when required.

Don't be ashamed: To ask for discounts, to ask for a longer credit period, to order *vada - pavs* instead of pizzas for your team when they work late, to take pay cuts, to fix small problems on your own - Do not hesitate.

Keep your word: Never break the trust of your team, any customer, or vendor. If you cannot keep your word because of some reason and things didn't go as per the plan - make sure you communicate. And do not forget to make up for it later.

I could be thought of as an 'old school' with my thoughts. I am not against the scale and big valuations, but I prefer to see invested money making more money, which, in turn, would attract more funding. After all, isn't *MAKING MONEY* rule #1 for a successful business even if it is a startup?

PostScript 6: We were in talks to acquire a big international property portal to boost the traffic and audience for Gemideals.com and the marketing platform for our upcoming real estate projects. At a discounted valuation, it made sense to acquire the brand and ride on its popularity to raise funds for the company. But as we deep-dived into their operations, it made us realize that taking over their debt wouldn't be prudent at that time for our business. And we chickened out at that time, thinking that being lean and making it big later would be a better path.

CHAPTER 7

Lessons By Dad

Post adolescence one of the most complex and yet maybe the closest relationships that a man shares, is with his father; more so in India, where the father-son relationship is usually a nervous one.

The reason for this is that the kids who were born during the 80s have seen a lot of change in their lifestyles and this changes our general outlook towards life from theirs since they have had a very guarded childhood. This is where the disconnect starts from, and then builds on.

Well, mine was a similar relationship with my dad, where we didn't agree on most of the things. But that didn't bother us much as our paths never crossed which was more on purpose, as I didn't want to join his real estate business. So, I was happy on the other side of the spectrum working with global companies.

But the way destiny would have it, I had to land in his space in the year 2010 and we were, as expected, in the middle of the chaos of handling each other's expectations. My mom was the referee at most times, trying to sort things out and making us understand each other's perspectives. The next couple of years were not easy too, as we had a completely different approach to doing things. But as I spent more time with him, I got to know him more as a person and experience of working with him did teach me many life hacks:

How you see yourself is more important than how people see you: A pawn needs to see himself as a king before the world sees him like one. My dad had started off with humble beginnings, but as a family, we always have had a royal life. We never felt that we were going through a struggling time even if the reality was different. It was his larger than life attitude that made him do things for the family, which maybe weren't affordable at that time.

Be persistent, as it takes time to build a stable business: He always used to say, "It takes at least 1000 days to build a stable business and you have to be persistent to take the business ongoing through the rough path." My dad didn't have many passions, but the only passion he had was his work. But it wasn't the passion for the work that helped him build the business but the persistence for not giving up. I feel that if you put passion and persistence in a boxing ring, persistence will always win. Because passion would just love to fight but persistence won't know how to give up on the fight.

Don't take failure to your heart: This one quality of my dad, which I feel if I could imbibe in me, would help me a lot. He was a person who never flinched even if the thing he had put years of effort into ultimately didn't go his way. He would never take that setback to his heart and just continue working full steam ahead, nevertheless.

We should understand that in the process of building your dreams you may go through detours that can be nightmares, but one should get up and not stop working towards that dream. The fun is to start rewriting your story when you are being written off in the books of business.

When you play the odds with a backup plan it's not a risk but smart business move: When I look back and try to understand certain investments he made in certain projects, it amazes me. He invested in projects which seemed very risky at that time and also when the money required for them was not with us. But that didn't deter him from taking the plunge, as he always had an exit plan in case everything fell out of place. He truly knew the art to make money when you have none.

Kill the ego before it kills your good work: When it was anything related to work, my dad never had an ego. He never let ego come in the way of getting the work done. Even if that meant giving a phone call to someone he didn't see eye - to - eye with if it was something related to work he wouldn't shy away to call that person. Because it was *Work* and that came above the ego for him.

My one piece of advice to everyone reading this book: Beyond all the arguments and disagreements that you have with your dad, make sure you learn from their experiences in life, as that will help you build your life better. I think I am very lucky to have worked with my dad after being exposed to my corporate journey.

The experience of working with him for all these years taught me a lot and I owe a lot to him for my success in business today. And I am sure if he would have been there today, we would still have a lot of arguments and disagreements, which I miss a lot now. Those discussions helped me learn a lot of things from him.

❖❖❖

PostScript 7: I was never on the same page with my dad at most times. The arguments were memorable with both of us trying to get to any level to prove ourselves right in front of the other. I remember once, there was a contractor who wasn't ready to go beyond a certain price for small glass work at a site, my dad was not giving up on the negotiation and the work was getting stalled for no reason. I stepped in to get the price that my dad wanted and got the work done. He was amazed by my negotiation skills though he didn't say anything much to that effect. I never told him that I had paid the differential to the vendor from my pocket and made it look like the vendor had reduced the price for the work.

CHAPTER 8

Victims or Villains Of Real Estate

Call it Mumbai or Bombay, it is actually the same - even the land that its natives are standing on is taken by duping the sea. The land is scarce in this ever-growing city. Hence, the business of real estate has always been considered one of the most profitable businesses in Mumbai. Theoretically, what a builder does is buy cheap and opportunistic land to construct a residential or commercial building and then sell the space at a higher rate. This all makes sense as land has always been or made to be scarce in Mumbai, primarily due to various reservations and restrictions in the city, so your end product i.e. the flat or commercial space will always be at an appreciated price.

All was well in this industry till it wasn't too crowded and things were not as competitive. I come from a family that has been in this business for over 30 years. I was never allured by this business, as I always wanted to create something of my own, and hence spent over a decade of my early career away from this business.

Eventually, to cater to my responsibilities, I joined the development business. I found the experience unique as my perspective about the business had been that of an outsider earlier. But, one thing is for sure that a lot of things have changed in the last few years. The so-called real estate business that seemed lucrative is now getting tougher by the day. The biggest victim in this entire change has been the small builders who were once very happy constructing a building or two in a span of 24 - 30 months and cashing in on that to get to the next project. They seem to have gotten stuck in the rut of ever-changing rules and regulations resulting in projects being stalled and interest money increasing for the debt - ridden builders of the city. These kinds of issues slowly crippled the industry. And it is a no brainer to understand that these changes have an overall effect on the entire economy. It is an undeniable fact that the progress of the real estate industry is one of the keys to a healthy economic foundation of the country.

Who is to be blamed for this? From where I see it - you can't blame just one side or a party. Everyone who belongs to the industry has directly or indirectly contributed to this mess.

Did greed get us to the situation we are in? I remember, when I joined the business it was a merry time for the builders. New projects were getting launched every week and there were some insane schemes that were going around in the market. Even though the global economy was in recession the real estate industry in Mumbai was flourishing. The private equity investment in real estate was at its prime. The Mumbai real estate prices kept hitting the roof and thus made the dream of owning a place in Mumbai an even more distant dream. But in the speed of development & increase in prices, the rules were getting faulted by few if not many. This made the government introduce new rules to curb the illegalities, causing the fast cruising industry to come to a halt. Many projects were stalled due to the change in rules, causing an increase in the cost of construction. Builders had to pay more for development premiums and developers paid high interest to fund their stalled projects that caused further increase in the cost of real estate in Mumbai.

Still, becoming a real estate developer remained to be an in-thing in the business circles. Every second landowner preferred getting into real estate development rather than selling their land to a developer. Looking at the high returns, even other high - net - worth businessmen like jewelers, big auto dealers, etc. wanted a piece of the real estate pie. Due to all this, the land cost in Mumbai has shot up manifolds in the last decade and this has heavily contributed towards the spike in real estate development cost for the developer. Now, buying a flat in Mumbai city has slowly become an impossible dream for many. "I must wait for a few months, the prices will fall," is the most favorite quote of a real estate buyer who has never bought the house of his/her dreams in this city.

Increasing input costs and ever-changing rules in development has put real estate in Mumbai on shaky grounds. The pressure is building on builders to complete projects. But builders would always be the bad guys for the end-user - but are they really the villains or the victims? We can't point our finger on just one side for this situation and it is important to change the attitudes of the parties involved in the real estate industry. We do expect the government to be a facilitator of development in Mumbai, not a roadblock. If slow-moving machinery of the corporation catches up to the progressive speed through clear and sane policies - Mumbai development can definitely catch up to the speed that the city runs at.

PostScript 8: When I joined the real estate business we were stuck in a joint venture project where the other partner wasn't keen on taking the project ahead as his plate was already full and he was delaying the project unnecessarily for us. He didn't want to even meet us and canceled on many of the scheduled meetings, without informing us. I started to go and sit in the builder's office for hours so that I could meet him for a few minutes. One day, after seeing me coming for more than a week every day, he gave up and agreed to meet me. The intent of the guy was to delay seeing no real benefit, so I offered him an exit that would give him a good upside in the then slow-paced market scenario but with the condition to be paid in certain square feet of under constructed office space, constructed by us, in lieu of his share in the project. He probably thought I was a fool to give such an offer in an uncertain market of real estate. But for our company, it was an opportunity to restart the stalled project. It turned out to be a good turning point as it saved time of litigation to get out of the joint venture and complete the project on time which gave us certain liquidity in the uncertain future.

CHAPTER 9

Dealing With The Different Worlds

I saw a great opportunity in the mayhem that the real estate industry was facing. I also experienced that being straightforward and transparent in approach, and sticking to deadlines would work. I managed to stick to my commitments with my projects and gained investors' confidence. This helped me to get more funds from the other investors in the market. Our company wasn't facing the debt-ridden situation the other developers were facing and we were one of the select few developers who were debt-free in the market. Surely, this helped us complete a couple of projects in record time. Even now our company remains debt-free in this current market scenario and that helps us to make decisions without the dangling sword of interest hanging on our heads.

The problem wasn't regarding funds anymore but of drama caused by other characters in the business. Out of the stuck projects we had, the slum redevelopment project had a major hurdle of over 220 slum structures and over 1200+ slum dwellers to be vacated from the land and rehabilitated by constructing a new building on the same land. The slum redevelopment projects have their difficulty level as maximum despite the spread of Mumbai real estate as there are many claimed stakeholders besides the entitled in it. I remember once reasoning out regarding the issues in the project with one of the local goons, who had been threatening me. By the end of the meeting, he ended up sympathizing with me and my situation and saying that if I needed any help he was always there for support. It was really nice of him to say that, but I sincerely hope I don't need his help ever.

You always need to watch your back from these stakeholders and so-called well-wishers who try to get the better of you if you don't go by their whims & fancies. I chose a different and difficult path on most occasions and this may have caused more trouble for me in the short term, but in the long term, most of them realized that I wouldn't fall in line with their threats. Once, a big-time minister stalled my work on the site, followed by a call from his assistant to meet him in the evening as it was election time. Rather than taking the easy way out, I challenged him in the Bombay High Court to get a favorable order. It surely was a longer way than simply meeting the guy and sorting things out but it did help me, in the long run, to not get bothered by such threats.

When you sit back and watch a heated argument between people you will find the one who keeps his cool and reacts less to the provocations will come out as the winner in any situation. Being always cornered in such scenarios during my site meetings with groups of 150 - 200 slum dwellers on my plot backed by the so-called local leaders, I figured the best way was to not react to any personal comments and let them steam out their anger and try to prove their points as loudly as they can. When the other side gives up on provoking you and think they have won the arguments, you must throw in your relevant points and solutions which they never expected; this would get you the support of the crowd and tilt the support in your favor.

The cut-throat business of real estate did teach me some real-world experiences and lessons that are now helpful in building any kind of business, be in tech, media, or any other industry. It taught me how to act in business, especially when we are surrounded by so much noise and drama. It is important not to react, but to keep doing our business. As entrepreneurs in today's time, we need to know rules that can help build the businesses beyond the disorder surrounding us.

Here are some factors that you can focus on to help you keep building and growing, in spite of the chaos that might surround your business.

Deal Making: With tough times around, negotiating a deal for your business becomes critical. But, negotiation isn't about saying NO all the time but saying YES at the right time. In fact, never jump to a no in your negotiations. And many times, it is better not to have the last word in a deal; let the other side say what it wants to say, just be sure what is said is what you wanted in the deal. Keep the emotions away; it's not personal, it's just business.

Funding: It's sad but true that more often than not, a highly funded startup mostly wins over a better product. But being a top-funded startup in a category won't guarantee you being always on top; you get there by building the top product. Today, just getting funded isn't so cool, bootstrapping to profitability is the way to go. And sometimes the power to say no to a deal that will take you away from your core business doesn't mean you are saying no to growth, but that you are focused on your business and profitability. Ultimately for the investor too, owning a percentage of something means nothing if 100% of the thing is not worth something.

Timing: You might have to wait for the right time for an opportunity to rise. But then, when nothing is going your way, the only way forward is to hustle your way in. In a business, it is important to be aware of your exit point at the time of your entry. Because it is not only about starting it right, but also about exiting at the right time. It is true that to be a quick success, one needs to learn to fail fast. I have observed that when you hear the stories of successful entrepreneurs, most of them miss out on telling about the importance of the right timing.

Yourself: You will be called with various names and descriptions by the world until you make a name for yourself. It's not only the path you take but also the one you leave decides where you reach. You never know when you are about to disrupt things, till later when you have already done so. Ultimately, life is all about beating your best version and getting better every time you do it.

In 2007, we were planning to buy a flat from one of the prominent builders in Mumbai. We liked the flat and were excited to complete the deal while the builder wanted to go for a joint venture with us over our land in exchange for money along with a percentage square foot area in the project. I used to be a silent spectator in those meetings with my dad when I was a white collared corporate. I simply wanted the deal to be a clean one without combining two deals which could later cause confusion. And, we eventually found out that the builder had different plans, only after paying 50 Lacs to the builder as a token amount for the flat we liked. We were on the negotiation table signing the joint venture deal on the terms decided when he denied having a termination clause in the agreement giving him access to the land and also giving him a choice to delay the project as he wished. This kind of experience gave me my first taste of real estate as he proved to be a charming chameleon until he received 50 Lacs from us. I remember having a follow - up meeting with him in his office where he was determined that he won't do the flat deal if we don't go ahead with the joint venture one and on top of that, he called us 'cheaters' for backing out on the joint venture deal which we had not taken a penny for. This made me lose my cool and I challenged him to repeat the word once more and get slapped in his own office. My uncles who used to have business relations with him were sitting next to me and they all rushed me out of his cabin, explaining why I can't speak like this to such an influential guy. Thankfully, we never did go ahead with the joint venture deal, and eventually did the project solely, on our own. After a lot of effort in negotiating, we paid 25% extra on the decided flat price to safeguard the initial amount paid for the flat.

But this incident did teach me a valuable lesson in this shrewd world of real estate - Never react to the drama in a business, be an epitome of sensible action.

❖❖❖

PostScript 9: I usually deal with folks who are way older and experienced than me. Being someone who hasn't been in the real estate industry from the start helps, as it gives me creative and out - of - the - box perspectives. Also, there is no obligation of proving myself as an expert in front of anyone. In fact, I like to be a novice in the room when meeting people from the industry. I do not prefer to be considered as the smartest person in the room and also say it aloud that 'I don't understand the real estate business well'. This helps to get more information from them and know their agendas. No one will open up in front of you if you come across as a shrewd and cutthroat person. Rather, experienced older folks will ease out to your point if you listen to their viewpoint and experience patiently; this always helps me put my point forward in the end. When you can't be the smartest person in the room, be the most interested one to learn from the smartest.

CHAPTER 10

Just A Brick In The Wall

"*This is how it works! You cannot change things alone...*" I have heard this or something related, many times in my life. Not that I have always been successful in changing the other person's mind, but I never give up easily until I leave no stone unturned in the path. Many would agree, I don't let go of my points in an argument easily and I am rigid in accepting what is considered normal, especially when I have made up my mind. It may be true, but I feel it is rigid to see the world in a pre-set particular way. I believe there needs to be a new way of thinking that challenges conventional thinking. It isn't important that you have to get something right every time and put your point across at the first attempt; you need to be ready to keep deconstructing yourself at every possible opportunity to reach a better version of yourself. The same approach holds true when you are building your business.

Business Plan: Building a business and its model isn't a quick fix process; it takes time to chisel the art to its perfection. You need to be self-aware and self-critical to keep checking if the things you have planned are going the right way. Being lucid in the early stages helps you get to the best possible model for the business you are in. It is true to an extent that your journey is decided on the basis of the decisions you are taking at the current moment, but that doesn't mean that after some steps in the journey if you realize you are not on the correct path, you cannot deviate your path to correct yourself.

Back-up plan: What you have planned for

most often doesn't happen. And then we are taken aback by surprise and lose the rhythm of the flow of our work. In these situations, we create more problems around ourselves, than solutions. It is more important on how you handle your plan B in the mayday situation than what was earlier planned and brainstormed. In hindsight, I have realized it is always better to have more than one back up plan and be mentally prepared to adapt and act according to what the situation demands.

Pivoting: Pivot is a kind of a correction that you need in the journey you are in, most importantly, during the times you get to know what you had planned for isn't going as planned. In business, a pivot is essentially a shift in strategy to test a new approach in a business model or product, after receiving direct or indirect feedback from the market over time. Pivoting is part of the process of eventually getting to the right model, step by step. We need to keep breaking and building ourselves in the process to find new ways to reach the business goals we have set for ourselves.

Secondary Source: Many times, you realize that the idea you had thought of was a great one but the timing for the idea wasn't that great. In case you think that the idea needs a while before it could get accepted by the audience, you need to build a secondary source of income around the business that can support and fund you before the primary one takes off. The common mistake is that revenue generation is taken very lightly by startups in their early stages. I guess that causes a lot of money to drain quickly, and by the time the startup has found its groove, too much money gets misspent.

Wishful Thinking: The attribution of reality to what one wishes to be true or the tenuous justification of what one believes in, is to a smaller extent due to the culprit called 'Baseless Wishful thinking'. Wishful thinking can be one thing while the reality of things can be totally different. And if things are not going your way, no amount of wishful thinking can change that fact for you. It is prudent to differentiate between reality and wishful thinking at times like these.

Pulling The Plug: Some businesses thrive excellently after pivoting and course correction, but some do not grow even after that. Pulling the plug at the right time is the key to these kinds of situations. The longer you wait to do that, the longer you would waste your resources over something that cannot be fixed. Financial management is important, especially when you are in high investment businesses. There is no point in spending too much when you are not sure of getting returns in the long term.

You don't have to build a perfect wall from day one; you need to be focussed to lay a perfect brick that leads to a perfect wall, brick by brick, in the end. And, it is said if you are just a brick in the wall you cannot make a difference, but I disagree on this. You can still make a difference if you are a brick different from the other ones in the wall. In the construction business, when you are demolishing a wall, it is important to focus on a single brick or point that you need to keep hitting till the wall ultimately cracks.

Then, it becomes easy to break the entire wall down. So never underestimate the power of a single brick as it can make or break the whole wall.

PostScript 10: Gemideals.com started as a real estate startup, we gained some high revenues on paper in the first 12 months of operations but the actual collections of those revenues were only 50% due to non-execution or slow development of the residential projects that we had sold for some leading real estate developers. By burning our fingers in residential sales, we moved that model to lease retail and commercial businesses only, but then, due to slow movement of the market in this sector, it took time for us to convert deals and ultimately, we had to shut that too. But In the process, it did help us build a strong network of over 1000 active brokers pan India, who were connected on the platform. This indirectly helped our real estate development business by selling our own projects, keeping us debt-free even in the toughest of the times. But as a standalone business, we did not want to invest in the product further and kept it as just the marketing arm for our real estate development business.

CHAPTER 11

A Thriller Called Startup

Life got smoother with the diversification of our business with the co-working model, which worked really well and we grew our business every quarter at a good pace. Moving away from the incubation of startups, it made sense to us to invest in or build startups from scratch that we could handhold.

That's when we thought of starting our own venture Beckfriends.com. Some of the key reasons that made us start the venture were clear in my head:

Building a business of impact: I think there is no better way to understand a problem than facing it yourself. A few years back, my sister and her little daughter visited us in India from London and when they went back home, they realized that they had forgotten my niece's favorite stuffed toy in Mumbai with us. Now, though the stuffed doll named Miss Melody looked like a simple stuffed toy, it was a very important member of the family according to my niece. She didn't take this issue lightly and cried herself to sleep for several days. The cost to ship Miss Melody back home was coming out to be higher than the actual cost of the toy. That's when I thought there lies a great business opportunity in this problem.

Combining skill sets: During my stint at Google, I was overlooking the travel vertical and had developed a great understanding of the industry and its nuances. That's when it struck me to solve the problem of shipping by building a traveler powered delivery marketplace. The idea was to monetize the unused luggage space of a traveler by giving economical delivery options to the shipper.

A robust team: BeckFriends team is unique with a combination of my experience in setting up business for companies like Google &MySpace in India and my wife's who had stints in Airtel & Unilever in the marketing & strategy function; along with the young tech talents from BITS Pilani as co-founders. All of us in the team knew that we were trying to solve a big ambitious problem to create a big impact and change how people travel & send things. And we also knew it would take time. For us, this ambition was the fuel to achieve our success.

I was happy with the diversification of our businesses, and enjoying a well - deserved vacation in the summer of 2016, sipping a chilled beer by the beach on one Sunday afternoon while listening to my favorite playlist with no intermittent buzzing of my phone. There was not even a speck of worry for the next day of Monday; at that point, I started feeling the aftereffects of the entrepreneurial life. But then, the thoughts of my transformation from a corporate employee to an entrepreneur also came to my mind; the journey which has not been easy. It made me learn & unlearn a lot of things in the process:

Sometimes you have to take the plunge before you even start walking: For me, my dad has been the biggest influence in my life to take the entrepreneurial plunge. Knowingly or unknowingly, I had got his entrepreneurial streak at an early age. My dad started from scratch with zero backings. What I have learnt from my Dad's experience is that anyone can make more money with money; it's an art to make money when you have no money.

And before I knew it, I had to take a plunge into my entrepreneurial journey. This had helped me when I was working as an employee too, as I never considered it as just a job but as my own venture. Hence, jumping into entrepreneurship was inevitable for me.

Mental toughness is the most important trait while building a business: While good things can fade off with time, it is your perseverance that defines a unique and constant growth graph, irrespective of the changes and the chaos happening around you. How you deal with challenges in your head is what defines your path ahead. It is important to remember, it is your responsibility to grow your business and reach where you want; the circumstances or other people should not be deciding this for you. Sometimes things go as per plans, sometimes they go at snail speeds; while at other times, you have to start running even before you start walking. Abiding by your rules, routines and business goals, no matter what happens, tests your mental toughness and even increases it over time for you to make things possible.

Building a business is like running a marathon; ultimately, it is not about the speed but endurance: Building a business doesn't happen fast and it takes a lot out of you. Bigger the problem your product is solving, the bigger your business would turn out to be and it will take longer to build it. Businesses that are impactful in solving big problems take a while but in the end, they are valued more.

Most entrepreneurs get burned out in the process as the founders sway away from their focus. The initial passion wears off & what counts underneath is the perseverance to achieve. It is important to not *just love what you are doing but make sure you don't give up till it is done.* In business, like in a marathon, it is important to run and endure for a long time, in the right direction. The key factor is to not lose your mind's cool and judgmental power when putting your invaluable efforts into something. *Keep calm and build on.*

Intuitive decision making helps: The real estate industry was going through a rough patch. My hunch was that, in a few years, the business in the industry won't be as lucrative as it was before. The intuitiveness made me diversify the business beforehand so that we have various revenue streams of co-working spaces, startup funding, travel, and logistics. The diversification did help us to be a stronger company as we were not much affected by the ups and downs of the real estate industry in the coming uncertain phase(s). I believe, for an entrepreneur, intuitiveness is a very powerful tool; it can be more powerful than intellect. Following your instincts helps you go through crucial moments when you are not sure about the outcome.

Building a business is a team sport: I had learned an important lesson about team building early in my career. When I joined Rediff.com in 2004 as my college placement, I thought it was going to be very easy for me as I was better off in the digital world due to my prior entrepreneurial experience. Little did I know selling digital ads is very different from making websites. In my first quarter of sales, I couldn't perform well; didn't sell even a single ad campaign. My boss that time, a veteran in the digital industry, had handed me my first account from one of his old agency contacts. It taught me a lesson that at the start, you need to give a long rope to get the expected performance from your team. And you need to push everyone in the team so that you can win together. Ultimately, building a business is a team sport.

Avoid mediocrity in the team: The worst thing you can do that can be detrimental to your team is to accept the mediocrity of an individual in your team, which is, avoiding addressing the issue. Because, if you are trying to avoid the conflict in the team by not addressing the mediocrity shown by an individual, you are sending wrong signals to the others in the team. Emotions and preferences should be kept aside in a team and all need to be treated equally. The common goal of the team should be to achieve excellence collectively. And for this, there should be a common language in the team and all need to follow the rules uniformly.

Being flexible in the execution of the business plan is the best strategy for building your business: 9 out of 10 times a successful startup is only executing a failed concept in a better way. Your approach to solving the problem is the key. In the case of BeckFriends.com, we started to solve the problem of unnecessary costs of sending anything anywhere by building a peer - to - peer network. But for the network to kick-off, it was important to feed it with a robust business model at the start. Hence, on one end, we started with fueling the marketplace with travel agents who provided us with the travelers happy to monetize their unused luggage space. While on the other end, we had merchants who wanted to use this luggage space for bulk shipments. For the next steps, we were already in talks with a few top airlines where travelers could let go of their luggage at the time of booking itself and earn cashback on their ticket through our new product. This becomes a win-win situation for all involved, from the travelers getting discounted tickets, airlines selling low - priced tickets without affecting their business trends even in tough times; to shippers getting economical shipping options.

Though the peer to peer model is the way the marketplace will become eventually, building the business through partners has helped us grow the business. Also, businesses like Uber & Airbnb were also built initially on the B2B model until the peer - to - peer concept kicked in.

Frugality is an important ingredient in the recipe of success: It is good to be understaffed & hire people who want to go beyond their defined profile to learn. It is well known that when resources are less than ample, then only people or businesses can expand their capabilities beyond their comfort, and actually grow. Plus, frugality isn't the trait of a miser but its concept is devoted towards efficiency in using resources. A foundational activity to build a startup is finding the need gap & filling it with profitability. Frugality has helped us build our business to a near break-even point even when we are bootstrapped.

As I recount these entrepreneurial twists and turns in my head, I get back to sipping my chilled drink by the beach, but not just this; also struggling to complete the pending travel network partnership presentation in the next few hours before getting hit by the chaos of the start of the coming week. *Since Being your own boss isn't easy!*

❖❖❖

PostScript 11: The most common question from the investors after the BeckFriends.com pitch is "What if someone sends drugs?" We have answered this question so many times post our pitch that we tackle it through a 'verified profile system'. It is only recently after showing traction in deliveries through our partner network that the questions have shifted to that of our business model and growth numbers. This has taught us the best way to tackle the 'It won't work' barrier in your business, which is through showing strong growth numbers proving it has worked well already.

CHAPTER 12

Play The Hand You Are Dealt

You are not always given a fair deal, but you need to learn to deal with this. And how you deal with this decides your next move and ultimately, how the outcome is shaped for you. When I look back, most of the time, various things didn't play out the way I had planned; like, initially thinking to set out to make a career path in media & technology while being determined not to get into real estate whatever may be the situation. My plans didn't change my destiny when I had to step into the shoes of being a real estate developer. But what was in my hand was putting efforts to change the path, and merge it into what I want the outcome to be - by diversifying the business into something beyond real estate. I have always refrained from calling myself a real estate developer. I rather prefer to be called a struggling entrepreneur, trying to balance multiple boats in the middle of a storm. After all isn't entrepreneurship like building your ship in the middle of a storm, to sail to the shore of success? But there are various factors that are involved in fighting that storm.

Evolving Yourself: We are just a subset of our environment. What happens externally around us is not always in our hands. But what is in our hands is how we deal with something that is beyond our control. You must not blame anything and make it an excuse for why you couldn't achieve what you had set out to, in the first place. Evolving or changing the external factors is not in your hand but people forget that evolving yourself internally may help you get to your goal in the end, though with few detours on the way. But what is important is to keep having yourself in check regularly, so that you are aligned to the destination you are seeking.

Keep The Passion Alive: "Loving what you do will make you love your job." But I always believed, doing something with persistence would make sure that things happen, and that is more important. Having an imaginative bend of mind, I always enjoyed creative stuff, be it design, movies, or writing. But I did keep my passions on the back seat for some time, till I got hold of things and understood how to get to them on my own terms. But keeping the passion alive is important, be it not with the purpose of earning, but with the purpose of getting yourself out of the mundane activities of business building. We never hired a creative agency for any of our companies as I enjoy creating ads, writing, or making short video ads for promoting our business. This helped me keep my passion alive in the process.

Blindsightedness Isn't An Excuse: I am not a gambler, in fact, I am very cautious even when I seldom make bets. Maybe, that's why investing in stock markets has been very limited for me. I have always had an excuse of *'I am already in the risky businesses of real estate & startup building, why should I risk my money more...'* for anyone trying to pitch me good funds or stocks to invest in. The reality remains, I feel uncomfortable letting someone decide the future of my money, where I have very little role to play. Even if you are just investing a small amount in business, it is important that you have some control over things that are happening. Being blindsided with results at the end, when things don't go as per what was told or expected, isn't an excuse for losing money in a deal.

Skin In the Game: *"To be successful in business and investing, you've got to have skin in the game, a stake in the company"*-Warren Buffett. In our real estate business, there have been many times when there were developers ready to offer joint-venture deals, where they were ready to take the project to development without putting an upfront big investment and suggested generating funds by selling the area in the project. I have stayed away from such joint venture deals because unless one doesn't have skin in the game of the business by putting a sizable investment, the said partner won't be serious about the progress and outcome of the investment. Also, from an investor's standpoint, unless you have skin in the game, you wouldn't be able to tide the business or investment in the way you would want it to go. Sometimes, you would want to suggest a particular direction, but unless you do not have a stake in the business, your suggestions or desires won't be paid heed to.

Create Your Own Fate: Being a borderline atheist, I don't believe in most things around the concept of the existence of a God, but I also don't challenge anyone's beliefs in this. But what I believe is you create your fate as nothing usually happens by chance, and you ultimately create your own destiny by your own actions. The religion of *Karma* is easier to follow for me as an entrepreneur. The religion of Karma may sound difficult to digest for a more religious entrepreneur. But yes, someone entering our home in the morning, and hearing the serene sound of temple bells ringed by my mom, might perceive that ours is a very religious household. For our family, my mom balances things by keeping the divine powers happy. For an entrepreneur, being Karma-fearing is more effective than being God-fearing.

In the end, it is like how, on the gambling table, we do not control the good or the bad cards that we are dealt with and are holding, but it is about how we play even the poorly dealt hand well. So we should focus on doing everything with the best of our abilities.

PostScript 12: I have been passionate about writing from a young age, from writing short stories to short movie scripts until early 2000. Though not technically sound, I did manage to make a couple of short films with my brother-in-law at that time. But something that made me pause this passion, was when we were taken in for a ride by one of his movie-director friends who made our short movie concept into a full-length feature film, without giving credits for the same. Being a novice in this business at that time, I hardly could do anything about this. But it did make me wait on my passion for movie making for the time being, till I could do things my way. It gave me a realization that passion along with desperation isn't a great combination as you tend to sell yourself cheap in the bargain. Instead, when you seek your passion and you have control over things, you can steer it better, to a more successful outcome.

CHAPTER 13

Approximation In Business Building

It was the month of March in 2017, my accountant hurriedly walked with authority through my cabin door and threw some printouts on my table to look at. The look in the accountant's eyes was as if he had caught me stealing from my own company.

With my head down on the papers, skimming through the numbers, trying to make sense of it, I showed I could understand what the papers in front of me read. The accountant directed the attention towards a few subheads with the numbers that might raise the eyebrows of the auditors. As I recollected, these were approximation numbers that were given by me at the start of the year and they looked a bit off the actual ones, making it the cause of worry for my loyal accountant. Lost in the numbers, I tried to make sense of the madness and the decision made for approximation rather than exactness over time. This made me think like an entrepreneur: Does approximation make things easy or it is a dangerous method to run a business?

Bigger picture: Approximation, as we know, is the art to provide a value or quantity that is nearly but not exactly correct. Through approximation, you get to the bigger picture by being intuitive as you remove complexity. It keeps things simple as detailing can lead to the death of creativity and leaves no space for spontaneity and experimentation. Scrutinizing facts in business sometimes makes you lose the big picture. So, an entrepreneur needs to be open to ideas and discarding less important information, thus ensuring that the mind grasps the more important features than just accuracy.

Increases productivity: In the real world, entrepreneurs have so much on their heads and by the number of different hats one entrepreneur wears, it gets tedious. So, an approximation strategy can be a relief in the madness. Without wasting much time and giving the overall strategy that the team could follow is what is expected out of a leader and approximation of the factors helps in these situations. It is always wise to know what to overlook in order to increase the productivity of your team.

Moving Swiftly: Approximation helps to speed up. When you are building a business, you build fast and get things in order in the secondary phase. Then, it is important to be focused around numbers in this phase since too much approximation can make you lose the plot. In the details, there can be a waste of time too; so, one must know the art of fine-tuning between precise values and the approximated ones. There are always errors that can be kept in control with the approximation. Also, with things in chaos everywhere, in the startup world, you don't need to waste time with unimportant resolutions that can be delegated.

Negotiations: Well, there are two ways to look at a deal or a decision, either you scrutinize things and come to a conclusion or you can simply approximate things. The choice you take defines every step. And, I must say that in my whole experience, the art of approximation has come across as the art of deciding things not randomly, but with a sizable hint of intuitiveness. To decide things, it does not take only calculative analysis but also a certain sense of what is going on. This sense, one may call it sixth or seventh, is harnessed with experience and observation. An approximate analysis can often be more useful than an exact solution, especially during tensed negotiations.

It gets better with time: Approximation can lead to exactness. The more you use the approximation strategy in your work, the more you get the exact results you are looking for. By hit and trial, you reach a sense which makes you make more accurate and better decisions at that time and the next. Our minds are a small part of the world itself. When we represent a piece of the world in our minds, we discard many aspects - we make a model - so that the model fits in our limited minds. How paradoxical is this! An approximate model is a natural one that we can understand by default and excel in. It is organically open to growth with a better sensibility.

"What are we going to do?" asked my worried accountant who meant well for the future of the business. Getting the gist of the issue, I looked up and said, "Maybe we can just club the subheads and approximate to come to a conclusive number." Though not convinced, the accountant tried to make sense of the logic of approximate numbers in front of him. Ultimately, the accountant walked out of my cabin, shaking his head saying *"Sir, avoid using the art of approximation with money in future,"*...I smiled and with a relief tried to get back to analyzing the new product feature we were going to launch for our product next.

❖❖❖

PostScript 13: More often than not, I use an approximation in my business for most of my negotiations. I usually read the person on the other side of the table rather than focusing on the numbers we are haggling with. Reading the expressions during the negotiation gives you more information about how the deal is going than focusing on the words spoken. The aim is not just to win the negotiation but always have a win-win on both sides. One approximation strategy that works for me most of the time is when I am selling something, I divide the difference in the respective prices demanded by me and the buyer, by half, and add it to the number the buyer is willing to pay.

CHAPTER 14

What They Never Told Us

I do follow successful entrepreneurs and their journeys. Among all of them, like for many, Steve Jobs is my favorite. He was someone who, with his sheer brilliance of making a difference with what he loved, convinced people to follow his vision.

Once, it was past midnight and I was alone in the office. I had a video presentation with a bunch of international investors the next morning. The previous year had been very difficult as we were not getting the funds required for BeckFriends, mainly because the concept was new and something which a risk - averse investor didn't want to get their hands into. Trying to work on the pitch deck made me gaze at my cabin's wall and brood on a *"Your time is limited, so don't waste it living someone else's life,"* said by a large portrait of Steve Jobs dangling in my office. Stressed out and tired, I struggled to get ready for the important presentation the next day anyhow.

I started my frustrated monologue with Steve Jobs, "Well...Steve, that was the plan... and dude that's what made me take the plunge in my late thirties to live my life to the fullest. But what happened instead - I am spamming probable clients' and investors' mails, waiting for a meeting. Well, maybe entrepreneurship is a journey and not the end. And, I feel so beat that I hope it ends soon and it better be well. The rollercoaster ride I have been through in the last few years has made me realize that it ain't easy as your entrepreneurial quotes make it sound. I wonder why successful entrepreneurs don't talk about dark realities in their respective journeys..."

Self Doubt: You tend to doubt things around you and often yourself when things are not going the way you planned. That's when you realize things are not as easy as you thought them to be, in your head. Doing your own thing surely sets you free but you must realize that a costly price has to be paid for freedom, which you ultimately pay in uncertain times.

Reality hits you hard when you see your peers around you doing well in their corporate jobs and you think, maybe the entrepreneurship plunge was overhyped and miscalculated. It sinks in further when you stop getting replies to your emails from people you have been earlier working with during your corporate stints. I guess that's when you realize people hung around you because of the job title that your 'megacorp' company provided you. It's actually you alone who has to make sure that the person you meet finds value in meeting you. Everything else is just image-making or illusive living. You've got to live for yourself and your ambitions. After all, the biggest disappointment is not living up to your own potential.

Follow-ups: The one who said, "Smoking kills you," would have never done sales follow-ups. Getting stood up on a date is always a tough one to swallow until you get a far tougher one, which is getting stood up on a 5 am conference call with an investor who was in a different time zone. Sometimes, there is a lot of extra - work to be done, which may seem unnecessary and trivial, but these are the very points at which crucial moments are created.

Being a movie buff pays: It resonated with me seeing Captain America in the Avengers Infinity War ready to fight with himself all day in the Avengers: Endgame. That's when I understood superheroes are just normal people with supernormal will power to never give up. Sometimes you don't need a hero to save you, but just yourself to push you to your limits so that you deliver your best. It's all about pitching it at the right time, so keep pitching and following up!

Insufficient Funds: It might be the untold truth, but you may need to get funded in order to be taken seriously in the ecosystem. First - time entrepreneurs usually face this problem; they start out bootstrapping with enthusiasm to build out a perfect business but end up spending too much too soon. An important thing about building a startup is that the money you assume would last until the time you get funding is never really enough and none tells you that before you jump in to be an entrepreneur.

Building your business is like being in a boxing ring - Unless you don't get punched enough times you won't become a champion. And if you think you are hitting below par, take a loan; banks will make sure you are always on your toes and making money. And the ultimate truth is there is nothing better than making profits before you expand your business.

Leadership: When you are running ventures, you need to understand that everyone would want to have a piece of you. You should expect to be ridiculed, made fun of behind your back, or trash-talked to by people who want the better of you. Instead, use this trash talking to help propel yourself ahead and do better. It is the price you have to pay for being a leader. But you need to understand that you cannot be bigger or more important than the business that you lead, and you need to do whatever it takes to make it bloom.

I have been cornered by folks who wanted a reaction from me, probably so that things get out of control and I am blamed for it. I have been laughed at by many senior folks in the industry for being someone who has no clue and I have also been threatened by more powerful people who wanted me to back out. But holding my own sort in these situations has helped me to reason out with these folks, to convince them and see things through my eyes.

People: As a leader, you cannot ask your team to do something you are not following on your own. The best way to win the confidence of your team is to be standing at the forefront in the firing line with them. When they see you can do it, they can trust you to lead them. This works better than ridiculing them if they are underperforming.

But you also need to do things with the correct expectations beforehand, as you may not get results as you expected. You should be satisfied nevertheless when you know that you and the team have given it all in the situation.

Bad Decisions: While building your business, you can get stuck in many tough situations where too much time and money is wasted, even before one realizes what had been wrong. It is wise to go for 'how it can be fixed' as soon as possible. While growing a business it isn't important to be right all the time, but it is important how quickly you can turn your wrong actions towards the right opportunities when you see them.

Often the business is stuck between the difficult choice of letting it go or changing its path. And more often than not, entrepreneurs continue with a stagnated business model even when they know it isn't going anywhere because it seems difficult to accept that the model isn't working. But, one must know that going with the wrong strategy can lead to catastrophic effects and close all doors to newer paths and ventures. Sometimes, letting go can be the bravest thing to do and pivoting your business model can be the way you can save it. Statistically, bad decisions are only the second biggest reason for failure, first is indecisiveness. Always try to be ahead of the curve or be the reason for the curve to go upwards.

In the end, every story is unique and you are only working towards making yours one to be remembered. When you are building something impactful, it takes time. It's a long and lonely journey with tough realities surrounding it. You need to take one forward step at a time and try not to go backward.

"People who are crazy enough to think they can change the world are the ones who do." Steve Jobs knew this to be true that to change the game, you have to take the charge and others would follow. I have tried to abide by this in my journey.

❖❖❖

PostScript 14: It is not necessary that you learn from successful entrepreneurs only. You can learn from the unsuccessful ones too. And sometimes, being not that successful does not mean they're doing things differently from the successful ones. The difference is a matter of timing. Many times, I do follow struggling entrepreneurs around to understand what they did wrong in their journeys. The learnings you get from them are always more insightful as compared to that of the guys who have made it to the top. Usually, the difference between success and failure is the timing of the idea and its inception. So, I feel fate does play an important role in success.

CHAPTER 15

WTF Forty

'Screech...' I hear a yellow garbage dumper truck brake suddenly on the red light, releasing the grey smoke from behind which mushroomed on the windscreen of my black SUV. I stopped behind the muddy vehicle in time to avoid a collision. As usual, I was running late for my meeting; some bad habits die hard. My big fortieth birthday had recently gone by. I looked away from the grey smoke thrown at me from the dumper and in a blur, saw a guy in a black jacket and ripped jeans in a red color sports car waiting for the signal to go green. Disoriented by what I saw, I got into a thought of how this could have been me, and the circumstances that didn't make me the carefree dude on the red sports car right now:

The Indian Society: My parents never forced me to take up a particular education stream or career path. It was pretty alright for them with me taking a high-end computer course back in the summer vacation of 1990 when I was just 10 years old and not many knew anything about computers. They never differentiated between me and my sister and never pressurized for a particular career path to take. But in a typical Indian family, as usual, the complex Indian societal pressures and expectations from men are fed to them since childhood. And, when we hit our mid 30's, we realize we aren't comparable to the women and are definitely lagging behind them in emotional strength. But having been projected as superior from the start, we need to live up to the wrong notion. Accepting reality isn't easy after so many years of habit consolidations, leading to feeding the very fragile "male ego".

The Women Power: In our family, though my mom never got directly associated with the business, she was always the sounding board for my father and even for me at the times of crucial decisions. Getting her sharp perspective on things always has helped me to get insights that I wouldn't have thought about otherwise. Also sometimes, it is good to have someone who doesn't know the depth of the problem because then the person's outlook is not focused just on the problem and hence, a more open perspective could be generated for the solution. With her charismatic personality, she has always been the socially dynamic one in the family that has helped us be socially well connected.

My elder sister has always been a style icon for me. I always tried to catch up to her style and coolness, including the new things she so quickly adapted to. I remember, as a child, she used to listen to some cool English songs like that of Boney M, George Michael, while I was the *desi* kid who would listen to the Bollywood songs. But whenever she put those songs on, I did enjoy them. To date, I try to match up to her style and sense and that, I think, has helped me get, and even probably made me try to get a bit of extra 'voguish' from the rest of my peers and colleagues. Sometimes, I even got a lot of flak from those around me. Ultimately, your style is what you carry, but, of course, you need confidence for it and that gets imbibed in you from a young age.

The Fitness Regime: You have to be fit at 40

to fit in - Hitting the gym is in vogue after hitting mid 30's. And you know, what happens when you are working out or getting into a fitness regime? Yes, you guessed it right; you talk a lot about it. Randomly trying to get into fitness like a whim in your late 30's makes you create a lot of noise around it with your peers; how regular you are at the gym to the special crash diets to the coolness of running half marathons and whatnot. Sometimes being competitive makes things worse, especially causing roadblocks like slip discs to major fatalities due to overexertion and crazy diet plans. At this stage, consistent routine always works better than the intensity of the workout, and the secret code of eating right should be that of a moderate, healthy diet that is not strictly restricted. After all, fitness is not a race; it's a journey you need to enjoy.

You need to be self - motivated to be fit. I challenge myself in various ways, like going off alcohol or sugar for 60 days. That's my way of keeping a check on my willpower. I challenged myself to bring in my 40th birthday by doing 100 push-ups daily for 30 days, till my birthday. The milestone of reaching 3000 push-ups on the D-day helped me be motivated. And whenever I felt low on motivation on the journey of reaching the goal, I started putting my workout pictures and videos on social media which helped me keep going. It also made me realize that I might be inspiring people in this way. Many people joined in and it became a commitment to complete fitness goals together. Sometimes it benefits using social media; to push yourself to do better and keep the pressure on.

The Economical Twists: A typical Indian man faces a major part of the economic realities post 30's, as till then, a typical Indian man mostly stays with his family, oblivious of economic realities of running their own house. All thanks to the non - nuclear family structures. Everything seems in control until they are hit by it like a bolt of lightning. Repercussions include the need to move away to a nuclear structure due to circumstances, which further gets intensified after having kids. The pressure to match up to the ease and standards which are already set makes one postpone further and de-risk the future plans of doing things they wanted to.

Working with the spouse: It can be something that if cracked well, can help you build your business very effectively. My wife and I have been working together since the inception of the incubation business. Though we come from very diverse backgrounds and careers, this diversity has helped us contribute to the business in our own ways and we have learned to leverage each other's unique strengths. It is tough but there are certain hacks that can help to manage a cordial relationship at work with your spouse. You need to decide on a common goal, and check-in with each other frequently. And you need to maintain separate working spaces and work in different departments or divisions which would help you not get in each other's way on a daily basis. We work together in the co-working business and are co-founders in Beckfriends. But we also do not get in each other's way; she keeps away from my real estate development business and I do not get into the way of her Yoga fitness venture: PurnaYog.

The Surroundings: I really believe in the power of the surroundings; the perceptions do get created and influenced by them. After working a decade in the new media industry and the next decade in the real estate industry, many things unfolded before my eyes which helped me be the person I am today. My surroundings have contributed to my personality and my way of looking at things.

Many times when you are seen as an oddball, you are pulled down by others in the group to come to their level so that the equilibrium of the group doesn't change and the individual egos do not get hurt. This is also because people despise change, they do not want to change their ways of thinking. And even if there is one person who has a different way of looking at things, and tries to up the game if things are looking stagnant; this person isn't allowed to get to the next level. It makes sense to take a break from this environment and surroundings to get your thoughts clear and prepare for the impact you are seeking. One must be comfortable in his or her skin. Sometimes, when you step back you get the desired effect on people, making them understand the importance and the point better. And also, when you step back, you know your worth in the system.

The Friends: In your group of friends, often you will see that after a certain time there would be a set of people who wouldn't want to change and would like to have a status quo without questions. It's important to handle such scenarios in a delicate and a quick-witted manner as you wouldn't want to disrupt your roots and your connections with those who matter to you. Your roots are important for you to be grounded, especially when you are in your 30's and 40's. And, the connections are, many times, very important for an environment where you can get relentless feedback to lay the seeds for the future growth of everyone involved. But, be proactive to not hinder your own growth if there is too much push back for a particular change. You should resume the efforts if only things are getting too stagnant in your entourage, but don't ruffle too many feathers if not many are ready for the change. Find a sweet spot for everything to work.

The Perspective: Nowadays, we see a lot of arguments in real life or WhatsApp groups over issues, divided opinions and there are many who leave the group over these differences of opinions. Discussions go out of hand many times and many things are said at the moment, appropriate or inappropriate. I see this as a problem of clash in perspectives and when you are a third party in these arguments, you realize these arguments happen more due to not being able to see the issue from another person's perspective, which follows a difference of opinion. A life hack that has worked for me is to consider or follow an equal set of opposing opinions from people on the social media feeds; this helps to understand the problem from both sides.

The FOMO Effect: An average Indian male in his mid - '30s is usually driven by a fear of missing out on golden opportunities, like the ones he might have missed in his earlier days. And then, social anxiety builds up, by thinking one is absent from the more rewarding experiences as compared to others. This leads to compulsive behavior, even if it is just virtually on a social media platform which is actually meaningless most of the time. Fear of Missing Out or "FOMO" is mostly driven by the fear of having made the wrong decisions especially related to spending your time. This fear is not limited to a particular gender and has negative influences on people's psychological health and well - being. Stay away from negative people; two negatives make a positive is only true in mathematics, not in life. Also, the people who are not a part of your growth must be avoided; else it sucks up a lot of your daily energy and time. You and your dreams are unique, but we all are connected as a collective humanity. Hence, there is no place for any fear of being left out.

...I jolted into reality from the car honking behind me, realizing that the traffic signal was green already. While the red sports car sped away in front of me before I could know who it was; an untroubled version of me in the sports car or just an illusion of what I could've become if I had not dedicated decades in balancing my life, vrooming into a... *What A "Fantastic"...Forty!*

PostScript 15: As mentioned earlier, I consider myself a borderline atheist. For example, I don't even follow basic rules of not eating non - veg food on certain festivals or days of the week. In our family discussions, there are many debates discussing God and religion. After all these years, one thing that I have realized is that I am most driven by my business and that is almost like a religion I follow. A learning for me has been that for a businessman his business should be like his religion. When you are true to the business and similar are your actions in it that makes you the purest follower of this religion called Business.

CHAPTER 16

You Are As Good As Your Bad Habits

"Sorry, I am running 30 minutes late...see you soon"

Now, that's definitely not a great message to read when you are the one receiving it. Well, talking about this, I am usually on the other side. I am guilty of sending similar messages more often than I have hoped for. This chapter is dedicated to all those who have waited for me...including my wife; I ended up reaching 20 minutes late at our first date, 'I am sorry that I kept you waiting.' It is one bad habit of mine that I wish I could overcome but I haven't been able to. In my defense, whenever I reached on time, the other person invariably reached late. That may be a very weak excuse but that helps me pass over the guilt of being late.

It is the combination of the good and the bad habits that make us what we are. It is for us to decide if we want to overcome the bad ones and enhance ourselves with the better ones. Mostly, we see that people want to play via their strengths and ignore their weaknesses. This kind of works well at the start, but later, the bad habits catch up with you and could ultimately undo a lot of the good work that you had put in. I feel, if you cannot overcome your bad habits, the worst you can do is ignore; rather, you must accept them and work around the same to make them helpful. How could a negative behavior pattern, that dilutes your positive side, be useful? Sounds bizarre, but identifying them and being aware of them is a good way to work around them, I am talking from my personal experience.

Being Overcritical: We tend to be critical of the flaws of others but usually don't see our own. But also, I feel, it is important to have critics around you so that you are grounded to reality; I would rather prefer an honest criticism instead of fake flattery. I tend to be over-critical towards my own self and also of people around me. And this seeking for perfection and being critical makes me sometimes miss enjoying the smaller, important moments of life. The urge to make things perfect ends up making me run after the smaller faults, ignoring the bigger things around it. Knowing this as a negative trait, I have consciously let go of situations for it to find its own solution. Sometimes, stepping back helps because, maybe, the solution you are trying to find is not with you and the right person takes the problem to its right solution.

Low Patience: It is said, patience is the key element for success. But I suffer from a constant 'need of change' syndrome where I would like to see the results happening quickly without giving certain aspects the time to settle in. This sometimes helps me to adapt to change quickly but doesn't give time for things to settle, and take its natural course. Many times, in our startups, I have suggested pivoting to a business model without giving a decent run to the model which was thought of earlier. One way of dealing with such scenarios is to stop keeping track of the progress for a while and get back to it after a set time has passed, before jumping to the conclusion that something is broken upfront.

Driven only by challenges: It is good to be

driven by challenges, but it may not be good to react whenever challenged, especially when you're told that 'you can't do it'. Well, that's a trait that sometimes pushes me to do things; some positives like pushing myself to do a tough task might come out of it. But, sometimes, while I try to prove myself, it makes me do certain things that I may not be very proud of. More often than not, I have delayed certain decisions because it wasn't challenging enough for me to act on. Even, sometimes, I would simply put myself in an argument to get myself fired up so that I push myself to do the best. It is good to be driven by challenges but moving to the limits just for the sake of proving yourself can put you in an unwarranted pressure.

Love for the last-minute chaos: Doing things at the last minute is a trait that I would definitely like to change, but it is easier said than done. The last-minute adrenaline rush makes me think out of the box and do things that I wouldn't do in a planned manner. I remember, in my sales days, I used to make presentations for the client at the very last minute, sitting at the back of a taxi. Making the presentation minutes before entering the client's office made me chaotic in the head, which also made me look at the pitch in a different format. I wouldn't recommend one to follow this process unless they are sure to handle the chaos and pressure, along with its madness. But sometimes, meeting the last-minute deadlines can be the ultimate inspiration for you to push yourself. To overcome this, I try to maintain an annual goal list, broken down into monthly targets which then make my daily task list.

Low Emotional Quotient: In today's fast-moving business world, you often see a lack of capability in individuals to recognize their own emotions and those of others, and discern between different feelings and label them appropriately. This low emotional quotient makes one empathize less with other situations, though in my case, when I was aware of this lacking, I made sure I would be more self-aware of this shortfall, then on. The world, right now, needs more empathy than sympathy. More often than not, being a good listener is good enough for the other person to find the best solution for him or her.

Reaching your potential may require you to correct your bad habits and the best way to reach that level would be to start acknowledging these negative aspects. The first step is to change them or if it seems difficult to change, you should find a way to work around them. In time, you will realize that stepping out of the comfort zone and addressing or letting go of those ineffective traits actually would help you find your real potential.

PostScript 16: Being late never really made me lose a deal, but I remember once starting early to have a well planned day ahead and being on time caused me quite a trouble. I had fixed a meeting with the CEO & his team of a newly launched online job portal, as they wanted to start spending big on digital media. Deciding to start my day early, I fixed up an early morning meeting at 9:30 am, and the meeting started right on time and ended fruitfully with a campaign budget of 50 Lakhs. But when I stepped out of the office, I realized it was raining heavily, and the roads outside the client's office had been flooded. I ended up spending the night at my friend's office nearby. I remember, the date was 26th July 2005, when the entire Mumbai city was flooded, receiving the maximum rainfall recorded and I also remember saying this many times after that night, 'I am not going to fix an early morning meeting and reach for it on time, ever again.' Maybe, yet again, I was finding an excuse to avoid being on time.

CHAPTER 17

The Dark Side

It is 11:55 pm on the clock, a dark office in the distance and you see a lone soul working on his computer inside the cabin. The screen light doesn't cover much around but does light up the anxious face staring at it. Just a few hours ago, sitting on the same chair, surrounded by his team the same face was beaming with a contiguous smile, speaking about the fast trajectory of development and the growth in store for the company in the coming months. None of the team members that surrounded him in the room earlier would've imagined that behind the confident mask he was wearing, there was this guy with a pale face who was trying to arrange funds to provide salaries and bonuses to his employees the next day.

This is the real dark face of entrepreneurship that none talks about; things that are crucial in differentiating between being an entrepreneur and being entrepreneurial:

Humiliation: We are driven by the horror of humiliation and as entrepreneurs, we may face it more than often. Some may be hidden like those of last-minute canceled meetings when you have already reached the client's office, of investors avoiding your follow - up calls, of being laughed at your vision or of being lambasted for non - performance in front of those who matter. But humiliating experiences can be the fuel to drive you ahead. There are enough real-life stories where people have used humiliation to propel themselves to success.

Insecurity: You will never meet an entrepreneur

who hasn't been in self - doubt, on the rocky wobbly path while building his enterprise. The truth is entrepreneurs are humans too, they also experience a burst of anxiety often; the art is to mask it up in front of the world and put up a brave face. But these insecurities can also be the shadow that can avoid you from being reckless. Every emotion has its pros and cons, it is upon you how to handle and manage it for it to be fruitful.

Greed: The selfish desire to overtake and acquire more than one needs is often the underlying feeling that makes an entrepreneur prosperous. Because, without greed, one would be indifferent to making an impact and the change they want to see. Greed can be an important stimulus for an entrepreneur to strive and make it big.

Dullness: When you listen to success stories, they almost seem too quick and easy; that is, one gets an idea, gets someone to believe in the idea, gets an investor, and then shows growth and hits the jackpot. But when you read in between the lines, that's where the monotony lies. More often than not, mundane and dull things get the better of you in the midway and then, the future becomes uncertain. In these times of uncertainty, accepting the dullness of normalcy and still working despite that is the best progress you can make for your business.

Hustling: Being a hustler may not be respected when you are someone who pushes your way in forcefully. But in the current times, the truth is that your talent can only take you to a certain point but if you need to excel in what you do, you need to hustle your way in. Hustling can beat talent if your talent doesn't hustle. Many doors would've been still closed for me if I wouldn't have hustled myself in them. It is rightly said - Good things happen to those who hustle.

Aggression: Being assertive is an important factor for you to survive in the business world where there is cut-throat competition. When I joined the real estate business, I got pushed around quite a lot by the bigger guys in the business. In my naivety at the start, I thought it made sense to be good to the seniors. But, I guess, it doesn't work that way. You've got to be aggressive and show that you mean business with your shrewdest moves. There has to be an intensity to win for you to win. You cannot be a 'pass - over', especially when you are competing in a very aggressive environment and you cannot always be the nice guy who tries to please everyone around in such scenarios.

Anger: I have, many times, used anger to turn around circumstances into my favor. I also use a grudge with a person or a situation to push myself to excel. But it is important that you are losing your cool over something that is right or something you stand for. I realized that whenever I was pushed around, it made me respond stronger. Whenever someone tells me, I can't do this or tries to belittle me, it just pushes me to do it more and prove my point. You need to find the switch that pushes you to do better than your usual self. It's simple: You have to make it what you want to be in this life, don't let others tell you or decide what you can do or should be.

But at the same time, knowing when to get angry is an important trait to have. You need to have an idea of how to harness this emotion. Many times, when the construction work was stalled at my site unnecessarily by a local goon, I used to respond to it quickly and tried to get to a solution but then, I realized these folks actually wanted me to do that, that is, run around for small issues so that I get angry, irritated and tired. I caught their strategy and stopped responding to their calls and drama which made them give up after a few times.

Desperation: When you have lost all hope and you are in a state of despair, you could take rash or extreme decisions. But you can use this desperation in your favor as it can make you not give up and leave any stone unturned. Desperation can be sometimes a great inspiring force to ignite your inner genius. I was desperate to make sure the dead-end joint venture with my partner gets canceled as it was important for my company in 2010. If I hadn't been desperate, I wouldn't have gone to the builder's office for days, every day. I did it so that I could get a window with him to talk about an offer that he couldn't resist, and finally help me get started with a crucial project that could get our company out of the sticky position we were in.

Un-emotionality: It is true that being an entrepreneur, you can affect many lives, help them build, and enhance themselves. But when you are emotionally attached to things and people, it may hamper the progress of building the businesses. In a way, you are being dishonest towards your work.

It is important to be not driven by emotions while making decisions, even if it means that it is not good for all who are involved but is unquestionably best for the business.

...It was 12:00 am on the clock already. The phone beeped with a message from the bank, "Your account is credited with..." and it was just the message I was waiting for. It was time to be relieved, re-energized, and ready to be entrepreneurial all over again!

PostScript 17: Many times the humiliation has been a key factor for me to propel ahead in my path. Once, a senior executive of the Slum Rehabilitation Authority cornered me on the technicalities of my project in front of a room full of officers and my tenants. I fumbled in answering him. Officer had an agenda to prove I was incapable of doing the project and I didn't have technical know-how; he actually achieved his goal. But, having been caught red in the face in front of so many people who were laughing on my limited knowledge of the project made me quite determined to do the project and never be in such a situation again, by being over-cautious in numbers and technicalities expected out of me.

CHAPTER 18

No Entry - For The Unsuccessful !!!

"*You are not allowed inside...*" called out a stern voice from behind me, as I hurriedly pulled open the door to get inside the elite invite-only club of the city. Frozen in my stride, I thought about what made me confident to get inside this guarded entrance. In that brief moment, I started thinking about the rough journey and the factors along with it, which flashed in front of my eyes as I was standing there trying to be in this "successful only" club.

The Definition: Success is getting or achieving wealth, respect, or fame. It sounds simple but its meaning may differ from person to person. One may seem really successful to others but he, himself, may not be feeling that in the head. For the one who has the wealth and money, this isn't the benchmark for success; though acceptance or acknowledgment might be important. So, the barometer of success differs for different people, what is important is to follow what gives you satisfaction and what drives you. In the current times, the way things are, it is easy to judge people from outside and not seeing what they are actually seeking

The Clan: More often than not, we have seen worthy people trying to get a break into an industry that they may not be part of, or where they are considered as outsiders and the people inside wouldn't want them to even enter. This is relevant in all kinds of businesses because there are insecurities in letting a new person enter the space where the veterans have already established themselves, even when the person may bring in new perspectives and ideas. This comes out from the insecurities of the old guards as they despise change and want to be comfortable with the rules that are already set in. This is human nature and it becomes a tendency to safeguard their interests and the hard work of the years, so someone, who is trying to break in, has to put in double the effort to get inside. This is fine in the long run as that will only increase the benchmark levels for entering, and in the end, would make the overall caliber of the group increase to that extent. But, it is unfair if the insiders try to use unethical means to stop the worthy ones from getting inside. This gives an unequal advantage to the ones already inside and stops entry for the others who might be worthy of the place.

Showing Empathy: The successful is lauded and the unsuccessful is always looked down upon. But there lies only a thin line between them and at times, people don't realize this. Not showing empathy towards those who couldn't get to the set levels of so - called success is what makes people feel left out. We need to empathize with folks who might not be mentally strong and are, therefore, sidelined. The justifications like, 'this is how a cutthroat business or the world works' are bizarre and we might not know that we could be a part of the problem. If there is zero empathy for those who are vulnerable and who have lesser mental toughness than you, we are creating a dangerous world.

Being Humble: If you think getting to success is difficult, you must know that handling success is equally difficult. When you are on the path of building something successful, you tend to face a lot of flak from people in the journey along with the disappointment of failures on your way. So, when you reach there, you think the world needs to know about it, and in the bargain; you might lose the humility to handle the success. It is important to stay humble as success can be a fickle state to be in, while being humble will help you stay there for longer. And, in the end, if you are feeling invincible and on top of the world from where you can achieve any target set for you, you can do what I usually do– Just go and visit your chartered accountant, he will surely bring you back to Earth.

Failure After Success: When you have not tasted success, you become oblivious to the issues surrounding it. But if you are used to seeing success over a period of time, your bandwidth to absorb failure diminishes. The failures after a string of success are most difficult for someone and can lead to the person blaming others for it, rather than himself. Handling failures after success is the key to maintaining it. Doubting yourself for it and dropping your level of confidence can lead you to believe that you wouldn't be able to get to that pinnacle again. Your comeback is what would define you in these times.

As this brief moment of reflection concludes for me, I find myself standing outside that entry door. I looked back at the stern-voiced manager of the club who was stopping me to get inside, and I smiled. The manager was taken aback seeing that the person who smiled back was none other than the guest speaker, who was about to take the stage for, "How to manage failure in uncertain times" for the club's elite members waiting inside.

PostScript 18: Real Estate business is synonymous with land disputes. We have faced many disputes in our company, including one which ran for over 3 decades over a small land at a prime location in Mumbai that recently got settled by paying out the amount in a court settlement. When I look back, this dispute didn't have much to do with money, but more to do with ego-wars amid the parties involved. When the land was bought by us, I was a toddler, while the ones we were dealing with were big names in the industry. When I sat across them, last year, to settle the deal with one of the main disputers who was around 65-year-old, he humiliated me and challenged me that I couldn't afford to buy out his share, and said that I was wasting his time like my dad who failed to settle this dispute in over 30 years. I didn't say much at that time as the people in the room were very senior to me. It was a sweet deal for me to settle this long dispute in court within six months by paying them their share in one stroke. The said person did shake hands with me outside the court with slightly moist eyes. Though there were no apologies for his earlier behavior, I had got my sweet payback at that moment.

CHAPTER 19

End Of The World Or Just Another Day

The business has surely been slow since the last few quarters, and with the Corona pandemic slowly weaving a web around the globe. The last few months reached their lowest, making sure the year 2020 and ahead is going to be a dull affair. With the deadly virus and pandemic in the air, there looms uncertainty and darkness in the future. "Our greatest glory is not in 'Never falling', but in rising every time we fall." - says Batman. Trying to absorb the positive thoughts in the current dull scenario, I try to reflect on the situation and what an entrepreneur can do differently to overcome the tough times:

Discipline: When things are out of your control and it is the same for everyone, it is very easy to be in a switched off mode because the rat race is no longer going on outside. However, what can differentiate you from the others in similar scenarios is the discipline you imbibe. You need to wake up and reel in the regular routine that can take you through this dead period. Discipline is the thread that takes you from goals to accomplishments, and in tough times like these, the discipline thread needs to be strong as you would probably lack the willpower that helps you get going. It is all about using your time wisely. Discipline with sharp focus is the key to sustain in this situation.

Innovators: An innovation is a new idea; emulating creative thoughts and new imaginations to form a device or method. An innovator needs a stimulus to get to this creative stage. Especially in a situation where things aren't working normally as they should, innovators are more likely to get to new ideas or methods. The best work comes out when you are pushed to the brim when the usual methods don't work in an abnormal situation. I won't be surprised if we come across many innovative breakthrough ideas in the period of lockdown & self - distancing. As Thomas Edison had said, "There's a way to do it better, find it."

Stay on your word: In tough times like these, when we are facing the phase post the COVID - 19 Pandemic, your word is the most valuable thing. It is easy to make an excuse and deny or delay commitments, but when you honor them you don't just win trust, you win the person. It is important you never break the trust of your team, customers, or vendors in such crucial times. And if you couldn't keep your word because of some reason or things didn't go as per plan - make sure you communicate. And do not forget to make up for it later. In these times, the true guiding light of life is to do what is fair.

Take the risk: When the going is tough, many shy away from taking the risk. A pessimist always sees the difficulty in every opportunity; an optimist sees the opportunity in every difficulty. It is an opportunity when there is less competition around. At times like these, you need to choose between going ahead and do the unusual or just settle, and be ordinary. You need to exit the herd mentality, its comfort zone, and be uncomfortable for a while. You never can tell when bad luck may turn out to be good luck. But also, once you have reached stability, there is no point being carried away. It proves wise to be prudent, cautious, and safe to sustain yourself to the level you have achieved. So, it is important to know when to stand back and when to move forward in such times.

Opportunity in change: When things are at the status quo and aren't moving anywhere, then all things are the same level for everyone around. And there lies a great opportunity in these times as everyone would be starting from the same situation. The old slate might be wiped out by now. In the midst of chaos, there is also an opportunity to change - those who can adapt to this change can survive. This clean slate is an opportunity to reboot and get back to the starting point for all. There is a great opportunity for the digitization of things and adapting to the change that might have taken longer to accept for a few sectors. We have already seen the spike in online education in the situation of the pandemic. There are untapped opportunities in the digitization of things. The pandemic can act as the tipping point for the digital platform and services, which we all had been waiting for. Work from home and fitness is a big business opportunity for various products and service providers too. One must think out of the box to tap on the potential of any situation.

Willpower: An important factor in walking the tough path is the willpower to do it. I believe that will power defeats all powers. Your will power to never give up would make you go through the toughest of the situation because in your head, giving up is not an option at all. And if will power doesn't sustain all through the situation, discipline is the key to refurbish it for will power 2.0. There is always an opportunity to get up again; the choice is yours. Will power is actually like a muscle, the more you use it, the stronger it gets and then it becomes your character. Weak people do not lack strength but they lack the willpower to complete their goals.

Vulnerability: It is alright to be scared in these times. In fact, the uncertainty does put a fear in the mind and the fear is important to be aware of the seriousness of the situation. Overcoming vulnerability is the willingness to show up despite that, with no guarantee of an outcome. So when you show to the world that you are vulnerable to a situation, you are actually becoming fearless of the outcome. It is kind of paradoxical because showing your fears upfront helps you become fearless of the situation. Like, I always get nervous when I have to speak at a public event or do a pitch, but mentioning it upfront that I am nervous helps me beat my vulnerability in front of the audience I am facing and make them part of the conversation which helps me do better. Vulnerability is the birthplace of creativity, innovation & change; it makes you see things clearly and prepare accordingly.

Cheating emotions: Sometimes, you have to cheat yourself and build an image in your head which could be away from reality. That lie can help you pass through that phase and face the reality of the future. When my dad passed away in 2016, I didn't use his cabin in the office and kept it as it was for a couple of years, just to lie to myself mentally that he was still around and I could walk into his cabin anytime to get his advice on anything. This helped me tide through some really tough phases of my life too, where I had to make some crucial decisions for the business. I cheated myself thinking he's around and about what he would've told me to do if I had walked into his cabin right then. It helped me pass through that stage and come out stronger.

After attending many webinars on the topic of business post COVID - 19, I can safely say none really knows anything but everyone found it fun predicting because of being bored at home. Because, what can go wrong will go wrong and in fact, a little more than expected, so all must be prepared accordingly. Everything is unpredictable like this situation has been. It is your skill that would help you make decisions dynamically, as per the situation afterward. It may be the end of the normal world as we know it, but you will be alright if you are not waiting for a messiah to come and save you from the mess. In fact, What if the messiah we all are waiting for is counting on us to save the situation?

PostScript 19: Being fair begins at home, I strongly follow this. I have seen, during the pandemic, many companies contributed to the funds in the month of March 2020 and made a lot of noise around it. But, they also did cut the salary of staff by 50% next month. I felt this was a masterstroke by accounting and public relations departments of these companies. We chose to stay away and made sure our employees get paid in full in this hour of crisis. I would rather help my own first before I step out to help others. In times like these, you shouldn't deter from doing what is fair and must stand by your people.

CHAPTER 20

'Living The Moment' Makes You What You Are!

In today's race, we think excessively. And, most importantly, we have a tendency to want more than what we really need. When we reach a goal or something we want, we are still hungry to want more without enjoying being present in the moment. This becomes a vicious cycle. So, it is crucial, in the current times of uncertainty, to wake up and realize that the present moment is the only thing that we may have, and therefore, we should live it to the fullest.

Handling the outcome: The outcome of your decisions is not in your hand. It is important to not get too dejected with failure or overconfident with your long streak of success. You tend to start spiraling down a downfall if you cannot accept the failures or successes in your stride in the long term. Managing yourself and your ventures in today's tough times of adversities is a key deciding factor; the higher is your adversity quotient, the better you can deal with adversities in life. You need to be resilient at times, when things are not going your way.

The competitive race: We all are trying to run a rat race and some of us are smart enough to know that even if we win the race, we would still be a rat. But even after knowing this, we continue to be dumb enough to keep running. In between this, we don't enjoy the moments that matter. This cycle is never-ending. You feel that if you stop running, someone else would take your place and you would become irrelevant in time. The solution lies in being mentally peaceful to let go of this race and the unnecessary things. Living the moment and doing things at your own pace is more important than running an unwinnable rat race.

Self perception matters: We are always fighting the wars of perceptions as one person's perception may not be the other's reality. What must matter to you is your perception; it is important to observe others' perceptions, but at last, your perception creates your reality. So, it becomes important to see yourself as successful first, in your own eyes, rather than just seeking others' approval to see you as one. Your perception defines you; others' perceptions of you shouldn't. We end up wasting a lot of energy just to make others understand our perspective, thereby losing important moments that surround us.

Little moments are important: Reaching smaller milestones should also be celebrated to enjoy the journey to your destination. Life isn't just about the big life - turning milestones, but also about the smaller moments that matter. Your first job will always be special and your first deal is always sweet; while some moments may not be that groundbreaking in your lifetime, these moments will be etched in your memory as they are important to you. You forget to celebrate these moments to run after the bigger ones since you are convinced subconsciously that it would give you greater satisfaction. But the best moments, usually, are created unexpectedly.

Inner peace is underrated: We are surrounded by a lot of noise and most of it is unwanted that doesn't require our attention. Ignoring the noise around and focusing on what needs to be done would get you on the right path. This also helps you prevent making the wrong decisions. When one gets oblivious of the others and unnecessary things and looks inwards, he/she is more peaceful. When we talk about success, inner peace is never given the importance it deserves. Hence, many times, the success feels hollow because we have made it devoid of inner peace.

PostScript 20: We were involved in along disputed settlement with one of the biggest petroleum companies in the country, as tenants of our plot. We had already wasted 4 years in Small Cause Court trials to get the said company evicted; it was a tenant in one of the bungalows on the plot. Legally, we were right to evict them as they hadn't been paying us the rent for the last few years, but in one of the meetings with their officer, we got to know that it, being a government-owned company, has been given the mandate to go up to the Supreme court. This meant long legal disputes for, at least, 5 - 6 years more. This made me realize that the best way out was settling this dispute out of court. I asked the officer to set up a meeting with the directors of the company who could take decisions in this matter. Meetings of this kind required sign-offs by at least 3 directors of the company and luckily, we got a meeting fixed with them, within the next 5 days. I requested a window of 15 minutes in this meeting which was granted and I offered them a flat of the same square feet area at only the construction cost, in the building that we had plans to construct on the said plot. They agreed and we signed off on the settlement in the meeting itself. My dad thought the settlement was unfair as we were giving them a flat almost free of cost; I had to convince him otherwise. This was a key moment for me as the dispute had been delaying the project for long and we had already spent a lot on the land. The court's cases weren't going to be the solution too. Now when I look back, it was the right decision to take as we successfully completed the project and it helped

resume the long - stagnated activities. It helped the company grow and stabilize in the demanding real estate market in the coming years.

CHAPTER 21

Half Time To Goal Time

In the process of building your business, there is so much chaos that happens at top speed that you forget something which is very important - You forget to stand back and pause to enjoy the high speed in which you are building your business. Because, in the end, success isn't just about reaching your goals, but is also about getting there at your own pace. Contemplating your growth over a period is as important as moving ahead.

When you are building something that isn't built yet, you need to know that reaching one milestone is only the starting point for the next one and it may seem like a never-ending journey, sometimes. In the end, you might realize that work in progress was always more fun because building your business to success can be more fun than the success itself.

The key difference between success and failure of your business is in surviving the tough times. And riding the calm before the approaching storm is always more challenging; hence, here are few reality checks that might help you go through your struggle to success:

Entitlement: No one owes you anything; even when you may be from a top-ranking college or you may be coming to join your family business after spending successful years in the corporate world. You need to earn your place –I learned this the hard way when I joined the business. I thought I had an edge because, after all, I was the Senior Director with a NewsCorp company, but in the first week of being in the business, I was cut to my size when I was meeting the tenants of my slum project. It turned out to be a heated 2-hour meeting in a300sq. ft. sized room, overfilled with more than 100 people. We were nearing blows at the end of the meeting, but luckily, it didn't get that bad. Amid all this, I did learn my lesson. It was very naïve of me to expect these folks would respect me because I had come from a different, so-called 'privileged' world. I had walked into the meeting as if I owned the people along with the place. In the end, I realised, there is no entitlement; you have got to earn everything on your own.

After all these years, I have learned that success is not an entitlement and it needs to be earned every day. You tend to get arrogant when things are going your way. But arrogance can be a recipe for doom as it diminishes your hunger to learn and makes you insecure in the long run. It's easier in the start as when you start; there is no worry of being entitled to success as you have the hunger, appetite, and fear of failure to keep you in check. But when you taste success, it brings the feeling of entitlement; therefore you need to keep ringing the bells and rattling things so that you are very much in check.

Monotony: You build with monotony, not with your excitement. It's only through consistent actions that you get consistent results; because it's a fact that consistency always beats intensity. Since intensity might be for a shorter time, but consistency takes you longer and makes success a habit. The mundane things that you do to run your business from paying the electricity bills, to remunerating your staff, to paying the government taxes, is as important for the smooth running as the big deal you crack that changes the course of your business. If you doubt the importance of these daily mundane things, try not doing these dull things for a month and you would understand how important they are for the health of your business. Ultimately, it isn't the adventure that will tire you, but the routine. And, yet the secret of your success is found in the things you do in your daily routine of building the business. When your daily consistent efforts meet a high - intensity opportunity, the end result is a classy outcome for your business.

Failure: Failure is part of the game. If you have never failed, you have never been tested, and therefore, you haven't seen your best yet. A setback is only an opportunity for you to come back stronger. And during the time of failure, it's not your fans, but the critics who would help you keep moving ahead. Do not ignore them. You might get written off by your critics, but in times like these, you need to be the strongest rock you have always sought to be.

Focus: Focus is the most underrated F word in business. Ignoring the unwanted noise around you is the key to your focus. You should always focus on being right rather than being quick, especially during the evolved stage of your business. Quick decisions may help you grow fast, but slow decisions help you think through the options to avoid failure. Building your business is like making a movie, you need to keep checking if the scene you have shot is on track or not. Ultimately, without the focus on your future, you could end up with your past. When your focus is clear, your fear of failure becomes irrelevant.

Grit: Building from scratch is inspirational; scratching on till you don't get there is true grit. Because true grit rewrites your story when you are being written off and then your comeback will be more impactful than your launch. Battles are not won alone, but they don't end till the last one is still fighting. Hence, one must never shy away from putting the best punch forward. At the end, when it's over and you look into the mirror smiling it won't reflect your grit, it would reflect the result. We all need mirrors to remind ourselves of who we are.

Self: You are the byproduct of your thoughts. Ultimately, life is a search to become the best version of yourself and fulfill the dreams that you wanted to create. And if you have a dream, you have to protect it. The fact is - we all have the light we need, within us; we just need to follow it. Don't look back unless you want to return and if you hit a wall in the process of moving ahead, break a window on it, jump out of it and keep moving. Because the only way to being limitless is by pushing your limits every time and when you are limitless, even the sky isn't enough. The key is to be a slayer, not a slave. It is not about how you run, but what you run for. You need to be the light that leads not burns.

So, sometimes you need to cut the noise from outside to hear the voice from within. Also, sometimes, it is best to put up a poker face and not react if you are unable to beat the odds around.

There are very few who know what they want to do and even fewer who know how they would do it and usually, that's the bunch who actually do it! And the fact remains - success isn't just about achieving your goals, but also about getting there on your own terms.

It isn't about the destination but your journey that you need to cherish. Sometimes, you just need to see the situation through rose-tinted glasses to make the path ahead look rosy, even if it isn't, to keep going on. And then, when you have reached your peak you need to keep going, as you aren't great till you have outdone your best. In the end, it becomes a habit.

In the end, we all are what we are, because of our handicaps, failures & few crucial moments of life. The ups & downs in my journey till now have gotten me to this far and this definitely isn't the end. In fact, it might get tougher from here due to the uncertainty of the times that surrounds us. But I have realized that the important thing is how you take certain decisions in the key moments like these which would define your path ahead. In hindsight, these tough moments ultimately make us the real entrepreneurs. When the process of building the business through tough times gives you a bigger high than the success of it, you realize that getting to success isn't the goal... the goal is to keep going and this is only the half time to my goal time!

PostScript 21: In 2019, there was a crucial case in The Bombay High Court regarding one of our projects. The verdict could've gone either way and I was obviously much tensed about what the outcome would be. I was disturbed and snapping on everyone in the office and home. My wife was watching this silently and didn't say much. As I was about to reach the court on the judgment day, I got a simple text message from her saying, "You have given your 100% to this project, a judgment cannot take that away from you, so let whatever be the outcome. Be proud of your efforts." This thought has stuck with me every time then on.

Epilogue

When you look back there are only a bunch of moments that would change your path and take you to where you belong. How one reacts to these moments is what defines the person and his/her destiny. I never wanted to be in the real estate business from the time I was a teenager. I started getting myself equipped with computer courses that would take me away from this business, but as destiny would have it, I was in the middle of the chaos that I despised. It wasn't as if there was a gun pointed on my head to join the business, but I chose to do it. Maybe I didn't want to be penny - wise and pound - foolish to give up the hard work of my dad and settle for the unfair deals offered to us by others during our low period. Continuing my rising career in digital media at that time would've left me in a comfortable well paying position right now, but the decision in the key moment gave me a chance now to pursue my dream to make it big in new media & tech. The path may not be usual but it is quite a fulfilling one. For me, in the next decade, it is important to use my experience in the space of media, technology, and real estate to build further. What this diverse experience has taught me in various moments is unique and this would help me sketch the next decade. I would be keen to invest myself and build a business in these sectors, and use my learning to help people grow in the world of business.

Many times, our past dictates our future because we are not living in our present. We need to be completely present in the situation to understand what's going on around us and must not worry that things that have happened in the past would repeat themselves. We sometimes do not go into uncharted territory because we have seen enough failure in the past. It is a key that we shouldn't think about failure before doing anything. When you are tunnel-visioned about what you want to achieve, then you would not think about what would happen if things don't go the way as planned; you are just focusing on making it happen. It is kind of mystic to be in a mindset like this; to be aware of the present and not worry about the past or what the future beholds for you.

It is easy to look back and say that those were 'the' moments and they turned out as planned, like the ones mentioned in this book. But the truth is, I never knew how it would play out, I was just intuitive of the situation and knew what was at stake. In key moments, it is more important to feel right about your decision than thinking if the decision is right or wrong. As I reflect back, I would not shy away from making the same mistakes and taking the same decisions that I have taken in these moments of my life. Some worked out, some didn't but each was important to reach a place where there are no regrets; as I glide along the path to the next decade of this rollercoaster ride called: *Entrepreneurship*.

This is my entrepreneurial journey till now...to be continued!

Reach out to the Author -

Twitter: https://twitter.com/DeepMalhotra

Linkedin: https://www.linkedin.com/in/deepmalhotra/

Email: deep@imgemini.com